REFRAME YOUR LIFE

REFRAME YOUR LIFE

Transforming Your Pain

into Purpose

STEPHEN ARTERBURN

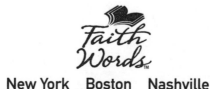

New York   Boston   Nashville

Unless otherwise indicated, Scripture quotations are taken from the *Holy Bible, New Living Translation* copyright © 1996, 2004. Used by permission of Tyndale House Publishers, Inc., Wheaton, IL 60189. All rights reserved.

Scripture quotations marked NIV are taken from the *Holy Bible, New International Version.*® NIV.® Copyright © 1973, 1978, 1984 by International Bible Society. Used by permission of Zondervan Publishing House. All rights reserved.

Scripture quotations marked AMP are taken from THE AMPLIFIED BIBLE, Old Testament copyright © 1965, 1987 by the Zondervan Corporation. The Amplified New Testament copyright © 1958, 1987 by The Lockman Foundation. Used by permission.

Scripture taken from the NEW AMERICAN STANDARD BIBLE® (NASB), Copyright © 1960, 1962, 1963, 1968, 1971, 1972, 1973, 1975, 1977, 1995 by The Lockman Foundation. Used by permission.

FaithWords
Hachette Book Group USA
237 Park Avenue
New York, NY 10017

Visit our Web site at www.faithwords.com.

The FaithWords name and logo are trademarks of Hachette Book Group USA.

Printed in the United States of America

First Edition: July 2007
10 9 8 7 6 5 4 3 2 1

Library of Congress Cataloging-in-Publication Data
Arterburn, Stephen, 1953–
   Reframe your life : transforming your pain into purpose / Stephen
Arterburn. — 1st ed.
       p. cm.
   Summary: "Bestselling author and radio host Stephen Arterburn reveals how men and women can see the past as a promise rather than a prison."
—Provided by the publisher.
   ISBN-13: 978-0-446-58033-5
   ISBN-10: 0-446-58033-3
 1. Attitude change—Religious aspects—Christianity. 2. Memory—Religious aspects—Christianity. 3. Pain—Religious aspects—Christianity. 4. Suffering—Religious aspects—Christianity. I. Title.
   IBV4597.2.A78 2007
   I248.8'6—dc22   2006034852

To Misty: You reframed my life in love,

my future with joy,

and my soul with new life.

Acknowledgments

My gratitude to Rolf Zettersten, who thought I would be a good match for publishing with Hachette and believed this book could change lives. Also, Gary Terashita did a wonderful job of turning my lame words into real, live, readable sentences. And to my able, competent, high-frustration-tolerant assistants Julie Crisp and Dianne Nelson, who help keep me together and moving forward. Finally, thank you, Misty, for your partnership in writing (and other areas).

Contents

Introduction   1

   Prison Break

   Prisons of My Own

   Potty Training

   The Mystery of Misery

   Reframe or Remain in the Misery

   A Reframed Woman of Faith

   New Light

   Tragedy-Trauma-Triumph

   Perspective

   History Repeated

   The Ultimate Reframer

   Whole Body Reframe

CHAPTER ONE:

"I Was Framed"   17

   The Plot Thickens

   Who Framed You?

   Framed and Reframed

CHAPTER TWO:

The World's Largest Barriers to Reframing Your Life   22

The Good Stuff Up-Front

What Not to Wear

Knowing You Need Help

Keep Me from Lying to Myself

WORLD'S LARGEST REFRAMING ROADBLOCK NUMBER ONE:

Stubborn Resistance

Lose "It" for Life

- The "It"
- Resisting Not So Obviously
- King of Stubborn Resistance
- The Stubbornly Resistant Heritage

The Antidote to Stubborn Resistance: Willingness

- Life Beyond Good Intentions

WORLD'S LARGEST REFRAMING ROADBLOCK NUMBER TWO:

Arrogant Entitlement

My Way

- The Bridge to Immorality
- The Adolescent Kind of Mind
- Living Like Royalty

The Antidote to Arrogant Entitlement: Humility

WORLD'S LARGEST REFRAMING ROADBLOCK NUMBER THREE:

Justifiable Resentment

The Most Dangerous Possession on Earth

- Personal Plutonium
- Petty Resentments
- Roots of Bitterness

The Antidote to Justifiable Resentment: Forgiveness

- Forgiving Without Limits
- The Process

WORLD'S LARGEST REFRAMING ROADBLOCK NUMBER FOUR:

Disconnected Isolation

The Perfection of Disconnection

- The Disconnected Life

The Antidote to Perfect Disconnection: Intimacy

- Imperfect Intimacy
- Your Right Versus What Is Right
- Dictator-Doormat Theology
- From Mutuality to Intimacy

WORLD'S LARGEST REFRAMING ROADBLOCK NUMBER FIVE:

Blind Ignorance

Take Off the Blinders

The Antidote to Blind Ignorance: Obedience

Roadblocks Summary

CHAPTER THREE:

Who Benefits from Reframing?   67

Past Hurt: Present Pain

Holding on to a Meaningless Hope

Exploring the Reframing Options

An Invitation to Anyone Stuck

Seeing the "Benefits" of Living in the Past

Assistance for the Disconnected

The Disconnectors

Conflict, Confusion, and Complications

From Potential to Productivity

Reframing the Largest Most Valuable and Powerful Number in
  the World

The Power of One

Discovering the Power of 1 Percent

No Way Today

• Ten Healthy Choices for an Unemployed Person

More Power of One

Reframing Emptiness

Deadly Drama

The Internal Reframing of Emptiness

Unresponsive Ailments

A Different Look at Depression

Opposite Day

Inevitable Dilemmas

Something's Gotta Give

Framing and Reframing Life's Tough Developments

CHAPTER FOUR:

What Reframing Determines   **107**

My Friend Brad

Stop Looking at the Tops of Your Shoes

The Reframed Mind

Reframed Relationships

Jewelry and Jail

Two Reframed Hearts

Reframing for a Healthy Life

Think-Feel-Act-Feel-Think

Whatever It Takes

CHAPTER FIVE:

What Reframing Is Not   **122**

Positive Thinking

Ignoring Hurts and Pains

Negating the Past

Forgetting about You

Staying the Victim

CHAPTER SIX:

What Reframing Is 132

You Have a Clue

Reframing Is Living with Deep Wisdom

Full Truth

The Frigid Wife

The Impotent Husband

Choosing a Creative Response

Prison or Picnic

Showering away the Shame

The Big First Step

CHAPTER SEVEN:

It's Not Always Easy 148

A Very Tough Look at Abuse

Sensing Evil

The Remorseful Abuser

Something's Gotta Give

Giving Up the Old Frame

The First Piece of the Right Frame

The Second Piece

LIfe in the Spirit

The Third Framing Piece

The Fourth Framing Piece

Putting It All Together

CHAPTER EIGHT:

Reframing Right Now 164

Hey! What Are You Looking At?

A Man's Right to Have Sex

The Other Side of the Bed

Using Truth in Untruthful Ways

The Other Side of the Coin

What About Your Right Now?

CHAPTER NINE:

Reframing Everyday Life 171

Traffic

Teaching Kids to See Things Differently

A Perfect Day Spent Inside

Avoiding Mr. Wrong

Daily Opportunities at Reframing

CHAPTER TEN:

Reframe Your Life Rather Than Retreat from It 178

The Frame of the Dark Side of Life

The Frame of Life

Give Up the Darkness

CHAPTER ELEVEN:

Reframe Your God 185

Born-Again Breakdown

God Is Not an Air Bag

God Is Not Your Overly Critical Parent

God Is Not Your Detached Parent

The Moses Model and the Messiah Model

Who God Is

CHAPTER TWELVE:

From Reframing to Resolving 190

The Hard Stuff

The Ultimate Upgrade

Living the Upgrade

Porch Parenting

The Process That Leads to Resolution

1. Examination
2. Openness and confession
3. Focus on now
4. Choosing to forgive
5. Choosing to let go
6. Making amends and restitution
7. Making a plan to protect yourself
8. Fulfilling the dream of reaching others

Worst-Case Scenario

When Is It Resolved?

CHAPTER THIRTEEN:

From Reframing to Resolving to Refocusing Your Life   205

A New View of the Future

Eyes Forward

Choosing the Point of Focus

Making the Best of It

Winning the Prize

The New Thing

Resetting Your Internal Automatics

Secret Powers

Not Just Another List

Simple Discovery Indicators

CHAPTER FOURTEEN:

Leaving You with a Promise   222

A Quote to Remember

A Verse to Live By

A Promise to Hold Onto

Epilogue   229

About the Author   231

REFRAME YOUR LIFE

Introduction

Prison Break

As strange as it might seem, four inmates in Greenville, Mississippi, were caught red-handed breaking and entering. While that is not such an unusual crime, in this instance they were breaking into and entering the jail they had previously occupied. The local district attorney said this probably was not the first time the men had done this.

These ingenious, "outside of the cell"–thinking prisoners found a way to gain access to the outside world. Police Chief Marvin Minor said the men did not seem to want out of the dingy prison there in Greenville but were just interested in making it more comfortable for themselves by bringing in stuff from the outside. They were loaded up with supplies of gin and marijuana for the long days ahead. And then, in addition to the original crimes that put them in jail, they were faced with the new charge: felony escape.

Prisons of My Own

The first reaction to this story is to think how dumb those guys must have been. Who could ever imagine a plot to break out of jail and then decide to go right back? Who would choose prison over freedom?

Well, quite frankly, many more than those prisoners in Mississippi. First of all, I have chosen to live in some prisons I could have chosen to leave. These were prisons of guilt and shame, anger and bitterness, worry and regret, and fear and anxiety. I have also developed relationships in business, ministry, and my personal life that felt like prison. Some of those relational prisons in my professional and ministry life were optional, but I chose to live with them. In my personal life, sometimes others chose to end their relationships with me, leaving me inside my pitiful little cell of shame, regret, and loneliness.

I could have changed. I kept myself locked up with beliefs that barred me from doing so. Ever said any of these to yourself?

"This is not my fault."

"My parents just didn't get it."

"Nobody can help me but me."

"I know how to deal with this on my own."

"I am not the one with the problem here."

"How could someone hurt me, knowing what a victim I have been of others?"

"You have to be crazy to see a counselor."

"Anyone would feel this way if they knew what I have been through."

"When the person who hurt me makes a move toward getting better, I am prepared to respond, but not until then."
"I am so guilty God can never forgive me, so I am on my own from here on out."

There are a lot more beliefs I rolled around in my head that kept me from a life of freedom, purpose, and meaning. I held onto those beliefs until my life in solitary confinement became more painful than the pain it would take to get free and stay free. This pain also led me to want to help others live free. While in college, I thought I had made so much progress with myself I should make a career out of helping others. At the time I had no idea how little progress I had made, how far I had to go, and how much more pain I would have to endure.

Potty Training

In 1977, I began my studies in counseling at a seminary in Fort Worth, Texas. For the first time in my education, I looked forward to every day of school. Very quickly I was involved in doctoral courses and providing counseling under the supervision of doctoral students. I loved it and believed then, as I do now, that I had found my purpose: to help people with emotional and mental problems.

Within a few months I wanted experience with those struggling with the worst of psychiatric diagnoses to see if I could help. If I could not help them, I at least wanted to be around them and experience their problems. The only job I could find was as an attendant on a psychiatric ward, and I took it with great excitement and dedication. I was trained to help the nurses help the patients in any way needed. That meant

I could be counseling a newly admitted person through his or her initial fears or cleaning toilets. In my ascent from custodian to chief therapist, I saw nearly every kind of emotional and mental damage. So many started on their path toward the need for treatment at the hand of a cruel and heartless perpetrator who ripped normalcy out from under them and left them with scarred souls for life.

At first I could not understand the depths of evil that were committed on the innocent. One man's moment of sexual gratification often came at the expense of a healthy and happy life of another. I still don't know what the accurate calculation would be, but there must be one somewhere in the universe. It would be something like one moment of sexual gratification produces ten thousand moments of pain and suffering during the lifetime of a victim. I may be off about ten thousand moments of horror or so, but I know one man's illicit pleasure comes at a huge price to others.

It wasn't just men who wreaked havoc on the lives of the young. Mothers did it too. Some smothered, even trapped their young to always be there for them no matter how old they grew. Never free to become independent adults, they collapsed into psychiatric care, not understanding why life was so unmanageable or their minds so filled with conflict and bizarre thoughts. Unexpressed rage and ungrieved loss piled on top of confusion and disappointment. These emotional burdens became too much to handle alone, so they came for help or were admitted by someone else as a last resort.

The Mystery of Misery

Every patient was a mystery. Was his problem perpetrated upon him, or was he born with a genetic predisposition to experience the downside of much of life? Had she had a harder life than others, or had she simply been less equipped to deal with the realities of life? In the extremes of emotional and mental dysfunction, the mysteries of the causes were just the beginning. Beyond those was the mystery of how some made their way to functional lives. It was astounding to see those who sank so far into the morass of a life of despair find the formula that would free their minds from irrationality and exaggerated emotional reactions.

What struck me most about these extreme cases is that if these patients could overcome what troubled them, there was even greater hope for those who were not in such bad shape. Relationships could be healed, inner conflict and struggle could be resolved, and addicts could recover. I have never quite lost the hope for change I discovered back in those latter years of the 1970s.

Back then, I was fascinated that some people succumb to abuse, trauma, and other harsh realities of life while others overcome them and move on to great things and fulfilling lives. Through the years I saw some patients lose themselves after great loss while others found themselves and new lives. I have watched broken people find healing and achieve grand goals while others never reached their full potential.

The differing outcome is often how a person sees life in light of his past and his current relationships as well as how others see him. Millions of people are still hurting over something that may have happened years ago. Rather than resolve the pain and move on, such broken people continue to live as if that painful past were a present reality. They judge themselves and others based on an event that could have been resolved long ago. Anchored to a past that cannot be changed, they wait for others to change in order to move on. The change in others rarely happens and not only are their emotions and faith impacted, even the way they look frames their lives in a negative, self-defeating way.

Reframe or Remain in the Misery

So many people live in defeat. They remain in their mistakes or the mistakes of others. It does not have to be this way. No matter how broken or hurt, every person can discover a process that will lead to healing, hope, and a new way of living. The process is called *reframing*, and its impact can be dramatic. Just as the frame on a picture either enhances or detracts from the beauty of the art, how we frame ourselves and the events in our lives determines whether or not those events add or detract from the value and even the beauty of our lives.

Reframing can be the key to healing if you have read *Healing Is a Choice* but cannot make the choices required for emotional and spiritual healing. It can be the key to unlocking your awareness and pursuit of purpose if reading *The Purpose Driven Life* left you feeling inferior to those who are actively pursuing a direction with purpose. Reframing can help if you have read *Your Best Life Now*, but you just don't seem to be able to exercise the faith and transform the thoughts that would lead to living a better life. It is for you if you read *Wild At Heart* and then returned to a mundane life of sameness and predictability. It is for you if you read *Captivating* and were left feeling half a woman and undesirable. Reframing is for you if you love the teaching of Joyce Meyer but just can't seem to implement the powerful principles she presents. This reframing process has been the key to new insights for those who have repeatedly tried and failed to create something new and meaningful out of life.

A Reframed Woman of Faith

Sheila Walsh, formerly the cohost of *The 700 Club* and now a Women of Faith conference speaker, is one who has benefited greatly from reframing her past. For many years Sheila struggled with depression that stemmed from a very difficult childhood. Her father was a wonderful man, and of all of her siblings, she developed the closest relationship with him. As he got older, though, he began to experience out-of-control rages with violent behavior. Sheila called these times "brain storms." For years Sheila struggled with the fact that the only child he lashed out at was her. It made her wonder if the love she felt from him was real or imagined. Fortunately, Sheila sat down with a psychiatrist who knew the value of being able to reframe events from the past.

After hearing the story of her father and her childhood, the pychiatrist invited Sheila to see the past events in a different light. He asked her to reframe the reality she had been living with. He told her there was only one thing that made sense of a father who attacked only her in the family. Her psychiatrist explained that her father knew her love of him was real and deep. He knew there was nothing he could do to change that love, which was more real to him than the love from others in the family. So Sheila's father, out of control and full of rage, attacked the only person he knew could handle it. He lashed out at the one child who would not abandon him. He knew she was the one most likely to forgive and try to understand.

It was a miraculous moment for Sheila as she saw the horrors of her childhood in a new light. She did not excuse her father's behavior, but she understood it in a new and meaningful way. Years of mystery were cleared up as she was able to reframe her past and see it from the perspective of a father who loved her dearly but could not control his own feelings and behavior. From that moment, unresolved pain and emotion were no longer a controlling factor in her life.

New Light

You may never resolve your past—or understand relationships in the present—until you reframe your past and see it in a whole new light. Reframing will help you begin to see a bigger picture of your life rather than just a shrunken world of hurt and a lifelong reaction to that pain. If you have lost your freedom and are trapped in old patterns that have left you hopeless, you can begin to live a new life. You can view your past—and your present—with clarity rather than through the lens of your heartache and pain. If you have never fully achieved all you thought you could or wanted, you can find a new way to break through the confusion and focus on your goals and your future.

You may have spent years trying to resolve destructive feelings with little success. It could be because you never reframed the events of the past before you began the resolution process. Reframing before resolving frees you to do the work needed to refocus your life, getting out of yourself and into the mind-sets and hearts of other people. It does not just work on the past. It also frees you from the horrible events that can occur in everyday life.

Tragedy-Trauma-Triumph

Almost twenty years ago, newspapers reported news of the "Central Park Jogger," a woman who was running through Central Park in New York City when she was raped, bludgeoned, beaten, and left for dead. She was found very close to death with massive skull fractures and more than half her blood lost. Her condition was so severe that emergency room physicians suggested to her parents that due to the gravity of her injuries and potential brain damage, it might be best if she died.

But she did not die. She lived and began the arduous task of relearning the simplest of life skills, such as eating, walking, talking, and writing. Her recovery was remarkable because she was able to reframe what happened to her in the park. While some would have personalized it, she came to see it as a random act of violence. While some would have felt the victim, she began to see herself as a victorious survivor. While some might have wanted an apology or vengeance, she needed nothing from the attackers. She reframed her tragedy, resolved the horrific emotions that resulted, and then refocused her life entirely.

Not wasting one moment of pain and struggle, she now speaks to survivors of trauma, rape, and acts of violence. She is an inspiration to anyone fortunate enough to hear her speak. It all began with reframing her tragedy in a way that it could be used to make her stronger rather than destroy her.

Perspective

Reframing is more than just seeing the upside of some very dark experiences in life. It is looking at the events of your life from a broader perspective than just the event. It is looking deeper into all the facts surrounding the past rather than personalizing the hurt. We carry some very destructive thoughts around with us that may not exactly be facts. We have a story of what happened, but it may not be the most accurate one.

Having an adopted child, I know that adoption can lead to feelings of rejection. And yes, there was some form of rejection that took place, but it was not as personal as many adopted kids think. If you were given up for adoption, your mother did not reject *you*, the person you are now. And the motives for the adoption were most likely related to wanting something very good for your life. The parent who gave you up probably did so with a tremendous amount of reluctance and mixed emotion.

Adopted children can come to see that they were not personally rejected. Their parents rejected only the concept of a child and all that a child demands and needs. It was *not* personal. It was not deliberate. It was a decision made by a parent struggling to survive and wanting the best for the child.

History Repeated

Reframing could mean learning more about the history of the abuser and discovering the origins of the abuse. In fact, the first time I asked someone to look into reframing his past was at a five-day workshop I conducted in southern California. That week I worked with a man full of anger because his mother took him next door, left him on the front porch, and abandoned him. He was in a rage because now, after all these years, she wanted back into his life.

I asked if he was willing to reframe the incident, and he said he was. I instructed him to call his mother and ask about her childhood to discover how she could have made a decision to leave him. The next day he came back in tears. His mother told him of how her mother had done the same thing to her, but she never came back. Now she was trying to be something better than her own mother.

Reframing the incident allowed him to see the whole event in a different way and have a connection with his mother. He was free to resolve the emotions around his past and refocus his life. During the next year, this man and his mother developed a deep bond.

Many parents and children are estranged from each other, not realizing that they actually share a bond of neglect, a common experience of pain, and a mutual battle to move beyond resentments and bitterness.

They also share a bond of anger. While the abused is rightfully angry at the abuse, often the abuser is much more so. The abuser hates him- or herself for allowing it to happen, for not getting help, for not knowing how much pain he or she would inflict. None of that excuses anything, but when you come up for air from a life of bitterness, anger, and resentment, you come to see that you did not have the whole story. The heartless person who hurt you may have found a heart, and the pain you feel may be that person's biggest regret.

The Ultimate Reframer

Many who read this book are Christians who read their Bibles on a daily basis and worship God in a local church. The central figure of Christianity, Jesus, was a man who spent his life reframing the reality of life. If people thought a small gift given by a widow didn't mean much because monetarily it was almost worthless, Jesus reframed the gift in terms of sacrifice and invited others to see it as one of the largest gifts ever given in honor of God. If men were pointing the finger at a woman caught in adultery, ready to stone her according to the laws of the day, Jesus invited them to reframe the woman in light of their own sins and indiscretions. When he finished his reframing of her reality and their reality, not one could pick up a stone to throw.

The most famous sermon ever preached was the Sermon on the Mount. It was a guide to reframing life. It was profound in so many ways, but especially in the way it invited us to see people and events in a different light. It says the powerless hold the highest positions. The sufferers will be given special attention rather than treated as outcasts. Then, in one of the most radical statements of all time, Jesus taught that many who are first will be last (Matt. 19:30). No wonder he was crucified after saying to the world that a lot of religious leaders who receive so much honor here will receive none in heaven. That was a radical reframing statement that characterized much of his teaching, turning the world upside down.

Jesus produced a shift in people's thinking, and two thousand years later, millions are reframing the world based on his teachings. While many try to work their way to heaven, Jesus said there was a different way. He said that rather than futilely trying to be good enough to overcome the bad stuff we have done, we should forget about it. He said we could not overcome our own sinfulness. He said every one of us is messed up. And he said that out of his love he would get us into heaven by dying for all the bad stuff. He said he would pay the price so we could live without all the guilt.

In his day it was a pretty bizarre thing to hear. Then when people saw him dying and those around him who believed him, it must have been the ultimate reframing of reality. Now we are taught about it in bits and pieces, second- or thirdhand. But to actually have seen the world's religious reality turned upside down must have been a stunning experience.

Jesus challenged the way people looked at life and each other. He would often say, "You have heard it said," then quote some well-known belief and counter it with, "But I say...," astounding those who heard him come forth with an amazing new perspective on something. Jesus' philosophy could be summarized this way: life is not all about you, is not all about your things, and is not even all about this world. It is not all about feeling good or getting what you want. It is not about what you think you need right now. It is about another world beyond Earth and an inner world of the heart without conflict or pretense. Jesus made a difference two thousand years ago because he challenged people to see things from a perspective that changed the way people felt, thought, and lived.

Whole Body Reframe

Reframing reality is still doing that for people today. With the publication of my book *Lose It for Life*, stories started coming in of people who were seeing the world differently because the world was seeing them differently. When they changed the way their lives were framed by their bodies, they began to see the world from a different perspective. Then we started our workshops, helping people work through the internal issues of the heart, the reframing became even more powerful.

One of our Lose It for Life workshop graduates discovered that she had been eating out of spite for her mother. When the workshop ended, she made a bold move to find out more about the history of her mother and how she was raised. When she contacted her mother, she discovered the emotional abuse was not just something her mother decided to do. It was a result of how her mother felt about herself and no one else. Her mother had been brutally treated as a young child, survived, and hoped to never inflict any pain on her children. But she did not have it in her to do anything but repeat the nightmare. She had never done the work our workshop participant did.

Once the overeater reframed her past, she was able to resolve the emotions around it and refocus her life on getting the weight off. She no longer needed to punish herself or her mother. As the weight came off, she created a new physical frame. People viewed her differently and responded to her in ways she never experienced before. This woman's new frame began to form when she discarded the old with which she viewed her past. For the first time she was able to view her mother as a fellow struggler, and it changed the way she felt and the way she ate.

In summary, reframing is the process of gaining new information and insight into traumatic events, both past and present, and moving into resolving guilt, fear, and anger. Reframing motivates you to refocus, move on, and live with new purpose and meaning.

For too many, a one-dimensional look at the past or recent loss is preventing their living beyond that painful event. Reframing your life frees you to live with less pain and conflict, full of purpose and meaning, and free from a past that cannot be changed. If you are willing to step back, take a second look, and do some work, this could be the beginning of a whole new life for you. If you are ready, let's get to work on creating some new frames that could make all the difference in your life.

CHAPTER ONE

"I Was Framed"

The Plot Thickens

"I was framed." It is a very common statement in fiction, movies, and even true stories about people accused of committing a crime. I imagine the innocent and the guilty are speaking that phrase at this very moment in thousands of prisons across the world. Most everyone knows what it means. When someone says, "I was framed!" you don't immediately jump to the conclusion that the person's picture was found hanging on the wall or that someone nailed pieces of wood around his neck. To actually be "framed" means someone took some pieces of reality, combined them with some half-truths, and wove them together in such a way that made an innocent person look guilty of something he or she did not do. Whether in real life or in the movies, when someone is framed, the plot begins to thicken.

In some of the more interesting plot twists I have read, the person being framed is often guilty of something and then the "framer" uses that to make them look guilty of something even worse. The man who is having an adulterous affair is made to look as if he murdered his mistress after her husband discovers her unfaithfulness and kills her. The drug user is framed to look like a drug dealer and goes to prison, leaving the real dealer free to continue his illegal trade. You see the framing plots throughout the writings of history and fiction alike.

Who Framed You?

There are other places where this concept comes into play, far more important than anything you will ever read about. It is in your own life. Yes, amazingly, you have been "framed." Someone, and I think you already know who, has taken pieces of reality and combined them with some half-truths and fabrications and "framed" you in a way that is not exactly accurate. Because of the lies that have been circulating in your head, you have "framed" yourself and made yourself look guilty and feel guilty about things that were not your fault. You have been viewing some of your strengths as weaknesses and allowed yourself to be defined by your weaknesses. If this is true, you are walking around with a very distorted view of yourself, exaggerating all that is not right, crowding out all that is good and strong and capable within you.

The opposite kind of framing is just as common. You have not made yourself look guilty for things you did do. Instead, you have "framed" someone else to look responsible for something that is clearly your own doing. You may be married to a fairly normal person with fairly normal problems, but you have "framed" your spouse to take the rap for all of your difficulties. You make your husband or wife look worse than he or she is to your friends and colleagues while you make yourself look much, much better. You play the role of victim and frame all of your life as a result of someone else's problems. Those you frame to take the rap for your stuff are actually guilty of many things, but they are not guilty of all the things that have gone wrong in your life. But every day becomes a new day to "frame" another person to be the sole cause of your own discontentment.

You might be reading this and thinking already, "This book is not for me because I really am being abused" or "This is not for me because the horror of my childhood is not something I just made up, it happened." If those are your thoughts, or anything close, I hope you will continue because I am very aware of real abuse in the past and living with impossible people in the present. I do not discount your pain for one second. Life for many is a living hell.

But I would not be writing this to you and for you if I did not believe the worst of situations could be helped by the use of reframing. Even if you were living within the worst possible abusive situation or the most neglectful and disconnected relationship, you may have "framed" yourself or someone in a way that keeps you stuck in a dark reality. You are not responsible for the abuse, but you are responsible for how you respond to it. Once you take that responsibility, you will find new hope and insight as you reframe your life and your relationships.

Framed and Reframed

There are several ways to look at the need to reframe all or parts of your life. One is using the metaphor of a picture frame. The context of the frame and the lighting of the picture have a lot to do with what we observe. Change the frame, and we can either make the picture look much worse or much, much better. Just as we frame a picture, we put a frame around our reality, and we view all that happens to us through that frame or that perspective. And as I have explained, we can interpret the facts so inaccurately that we make ourselves look guilty or we can frame others in the same way.

There is another way to look at the process of framing and reframing. It is with the metaphor of a building. Each of us is born with an internal frame of genetic strengths, weaknesses, and predispositions. Some have pretty good frames, and others are pretty messed up from the start. A person could inherit a disorder that could lead to distorted thinking or be born with an abnormality that caused others to relate destructively to him or her. Add to this neglect or abuse, and you find a person building a life attached to a very sick and sad frame. Everything is off-kilter because the building that represents his life is so badly constructed.

Amazingly, some are able to construct lives even with weak, crooked, or broken frames. The survival instinct keeps many people moving forward with great difficulty, but they keep moving. Often they believe life will always be the way it is. But if those people can go in and straighten up some beams in the frame, realign the foundation, and remove walls and the roof, the sky becomes the limit on the kind of quality life they can live.

In the remaining chapters of this book, we will change the frame from which we view life. We will reframe all the facts in the light of truth rather than assumption. If we can do this together, your life will never be the same.

CHAPTER TWO

The World's Largest Barriers to Reframing Your Life

The Good Stuff Up-Front

Have you ever waded through all the stuff in the beginning of a book to finally reach about ten pages that really speak to you at the end? For some reason people hand me a lot of books and say, "You really ought to read this." Perhaps if I were a little less forthcoming about my struggles, fewer people would recommend books they think will change my life forever. And the fact is, many authors have enough material for a really good article—but not a book. But they have taken the really good material and wrapped some other trite and true material around it and published it in book form. Thinking back, I remember doing that a few times myself. But this is different.

If someone has handed you this book and suggested it might be helpful to you, I am not going to make you wade through it or doze off before you find out whether or not you could benefit from it. I am going to give you the good stuff right here. When I started talking about the barriers to reframing your life, people started asking me to write a book about how to overcome these barriers. The barriers to reframing are also obstacles to many other great things that God wants all of us to have and experience. So even if you don't think you have anything in your life to reframe, you just might find this chapter, of all the chapters in this book, the one that leads you to some life-changing decisions and actions.

What Not to Wear

My wife and I love watching a show that is full of miraculous change every week. Some nights we watch three or four episodes as networks often broadcast more than one in an evening. Some of you may feel the same way about programs on The History Channel or Animal Planet, but our show does not have that hefty a pedigree. Our show is *What Not to Wear*, and we love it—I love it. If you have never seen the show, a friend or family member nominates someone to be on the show, and if she accepts, a film crew captures the fashion disaster wearing various clothes. Almost all of these people who dress so inappropriately believe they have a great sense of style. They tell how they choose their clothes and believe they alone know what is best for them.

It's amazing how people tend to highlight, rather than camouflage, the worst parts of their bodies. So often a person looks very nice except for, say, a huge midriff. And sure enough, low-slung pants and a cropped top shows off that belly. I yell at the screen, "You have to cover that up!" But for some reason they feel their style or identity must accentuate this most disproportionate area of their body. Why? I do not know.

It is so interesting to see the people give up their old attitudes and start to see themselves in a different light. They start to think about what the hosts, Clinton and Stacy, are saying, and then they actually become willing to try the hosts' sense of style. Some argue and go into the new clothes kicking and screaming, but eventually they get it. They come to understand they have grown comfortable with some very unattractive looks. Their own vision has become skewed and it is in the process of change that they begin to build on their strengths and minimize the weaknesses of their bodies. Often tears are shed at these dramatic makeovers, and we are crying, too. (Okay, *I* am crying, too.)

Knowing You Need Help

Of course this is a powerful metaphor for all of us who need to make some internal changes with regard to the "fashions" of our internal worlds. We are wearing some stuff that has been in the closets of our obsessive minds for too long. We need to replace these old "clothes" with a new wardrobe of hope and recovery. But we often don't realize that any better than the victims on *What Not to Wear*.

One night Clinton made a profound statement regarding this: "Sometimes you don't know you need help until you get help." I instantly connected with that. And I instantly wished I had said it first. It is so true. Sometimes we think we have it all together. We don't realize we need help until we open our lives to receiving help. Then we discover all the amazing areas where we can grow and learn and heal if we are willing to open ourselves up to help and to the truth.

As long as we keep ourselves in the same routine, not allowing new people to speak truth in our lives, not trying on new ways of living or looking at ourselves, we can continue to miss the best of what God has for us.

The reality is that when it comes to other people, we tend to have twenty-twenty vision, especially when it comes to the areas they need to be working on. I can tell you exactly how someone else ought to be raising his kids. With distinct clarity I can point out every little flaw in what he says and does. But when it comes to my own child rearing, I am blind to those same things. I just don't see it my own flaws very clearly.

To some degree or another, we all have personal blind spots that keep us from knowing accurately what the truth is and how to deal with it. Helen Keller once said the saddest thing in life is a person who has sight, but is blind. Ouch! Too often we are blind to what others plainly see are our defects and areas that need work.

Keep Me from Lying to Myself

I love reading the words of the psalmists (yes, there was more than one). They are profound and deep and often reveal an intense honesty that strikes at my superficial walls. I call upon the writer of Psalm 119:29 to challenge you before I let loose with the good stuff. In this powerful verse he cries out to God and pleads, "Keep me from lying to myself." I cannot think of a more powerful prayer to offer up to God as you look at major areas of your life. I have been able to lie to myself or at least keep myself busy enough not to look at the full reality of a situation. And so I ask you to stop for a second and ask God to reveal truth to you. As I write this, I pray that you will discover some previously unearthed area of truth and that it would open up a whole new course of growth for you.

Having prayed that prayer, I'll now give you the first huge barrier to reframing, healing, growing, and developing healthy relationships.

World's Largest Reframing Roadblock Number One:
STUBBORN RESISTANCE

Lose "It" for Life

Six times a year, I am the host of a nationwide intensive workshop on weight loss called Lose It for Life. New Life Ministries offers Healing Is a Choice and Lose It for Life workshops in a different city every other month. I do all the talks and therapists do all the breakout seesions. Each time I participate in leading the workshops, I am astonished at the people who have journeyed from all over the country to be there. Some have had to purchase two airline seats just to have enough room to fly. They have endured the embarrassment of asking for seat belt extensions as well as having people notice they are taking up more than one seat. They have paid extra for airfare, along with the price of the workshop, and they have committed their time to the event. Many of them come seated in wheelchairs because they can no longer walk easily, if at all. Oxygen tubes come from their noses because they are no longer able to breathe well on their own.

When I see these people, I think of the line from the movie *The Sixth Sense* when the little boy said, "I see dead people." It truly looks as if the life has gone out of all these wonderful people. You would think they would all be highly motivated to hear new things and try new ways of losing weight and keeping it off. But it is not necessarily so.

On the first night during the first session, I stand before them and make this statement: "All of you in this room have something in common, and it is not just a struggle with your weight. Each and every person here struggles with what I call 'stubborn resistance.' In fact, some of you have built your whole identity around resisting anything that anyone else suggests. If someone says white, then you will naturally respond with black. If someone says go to the right, you want to go to the left. You have a hard time going along with what others think.

"For some of you, the stubborn resistance is so strong you actually came here to prove you could not be helped. You came here to solidify your belief that you know everything there is to know about weight loss and no one knows you and your needs enough to help you. But if you don't give up your stubborn resistance, you will leave here not having heard, not having shared, and not having risked so your life could be completely different from what it is now."

I have never had anyone come up to me afterward and tell me he or she is the one person who is there who is not stubborn or resistant. It was not the stubborn resistance that made them overweight. That was a combination of the foods they ate, the exercise they chose, and the attitudes they carried. But it is the stubborn resistance that keeps them stuck in their overweight condition, framed in such a way that disconnects rather than draws people to them.

When they walk in the door of the workshop, they have an opportunity to reframe their lives by starting to reframe their bodies. But stubborn resistance can prevent reframing and feed into the belief that there is no hope for a new life.

Fortunately, because we talk about it right up-front, many who have held on to their stubborn resistance since childhood are able to let go and find a new path full of hope and potential. They not only lose weight and reconstruct their external frames, they reframe the negative internal constructs that have kept the need for more food than necessary at the top of their list.

The "It"

In their desire to reframe the outside, they come to see that there is something else in need of reframing—the "it." Most people come believing the "it" they need to lose is the weight. But during the course of the weekend, they come to realize "it" means much more than weight. As long as weight is the only problem addressed, the factors causing the weight will go unaddressed. So those who do well in the workshop discover the "it" they need to lose is the guilt and shame they have been carrying around since something extraordinarily painful happened to them. If they don't lose that "it," they will continue to feed "it," and any attempt to lose weight will be temporary and only add to life's frustrations as the weight comes back, worse than ever before.

But once people go after the "it" behind the weight, they

have broken through their stubborn resistance and are on their way to making real progress—not just losing the weight on their bodies, but losing the weight of the world on their souls. That in turn leads to keeping the weight off for good. (Just last night I met a graduate from the 2004 Cape May intensive. She lost and kept off one hundred pounds! Now that is a successful reframing of a life.)

Resisting Not So Obviously

Can you relate to those who so desperately need help but have a hard time opening up to the help they need? If you are not overweight, you might look at one of these strugglers and say, "How can a person one hundred pounds overweight stubbornly resist the help that could free her from her weight?" You might say that, but if you are like me, while my body does not show an obvious problem with weight, inside my soul—and inside yours—there are problems just as big that need attention. While it is easy to point the finger at those who have *obvious* problems, it is tougher for us to examine our own lives to see if we are displaying some form of this paralyzing stubborn resistance.

When you are stuck in your stubborn resistance, you may hear words from another but you refuse to truly listen to what is being said. You defend, rationalize, project your problem onto someone else or blame anything and everything for the way you are. Your life becomes reactive to those who challenge you, and you will do anything you can to protect the life you have created for yourself. You are not open to trying something new or attempting a different way of living. You are so afraid to risk losing the comfort of your dysfunctional rut that you will not take a look at how you could crawl out of it and live beyond it.

The Bible confronts us directly on this stubborn resistance in Acts 7:51: "You stubborn people! You are heathen at heart and deaf to the truth. Must you forever resist the Holy Spirit? But your ancestors did, and so do you." God, in the form of the Holy Spirit, is using the words of this book, the words of Scripture, the words of others, and impressions on your heart along with your own gut feelings to help you move beyond your stubborn resistance.

King of Stubborn Resistance

Perhaps you hang onto it the way a ruler did in the days of Moses. Moses went to Pharaoh and asked to lead the Israelites out of Egypt. Pharaoh resisted with all stubbornness. So plagues were sent to turn his thinking around. Now if it were me, I might have resisted letting the people walk out of my country, but after the gnats it would not have been a problem at all. The flies surely would have turned my heart. (One fly is enough for me. I know where those dirty, hairy little legs have been. But swarms of flies were not enough to break through Pharaoh's stubborn resistance.)

But if for some reason I held to my position, boils on my fingers and in other very uncomfortable places would have been enough. But this classic example of stubborn resistance would not budge even with plague after plague coming Pharaoh's way and being inflicted on the people he led.

We do the same things. We become the kings of stubborn resistance in our own little worlds. We get in ruts that lead us down paths that cause nothing but pain, and we will do everything but try something different. We develop habits and hang-ups we will not even think of releasing. We will hurt ourselves and those around us, essentially allowing "boils" to fester in almost every area of life. The boils grow and get infected, and we still hold on to our right to do what we please. Or we demand others understand the pain we are in and until they do, we will not budge.

We can endure so many losses and painful moments, yet still refuse help or even look at the possibility that someone, somewhere, might aid us. Somebody might know the way out of the deep hole we are in. But rather than look at the possibilities, we hang on to our right to remain the same, our right to live life as we choose, no matter how painful that life might become.

The Stubbornly Resistant Heritage

When reading about stubborn resistance, we tend to run immediately through our heads all the people we know who exhibit this trait, or we think about all the ways other people reveal they are stubborn and resistant. Those people are easy targets for the ever-pointing finger that keeps the attention off you and on them. This is one of those cases where twenty-twenty vision works on others but not ourselves. Stop the finger-pointing long enough to consider whether or not this could be you.

Now, let me give you a break on this. Most people don't come by this trait solely on their own. Often you learn it from a parent who has mastered the art of not budging. Some are even trained in the art by two parents who are adept at giving no ground or even seeing the need to. So often you are raised believing this is just how people relate. Each person takes a position and defends it. Anyone suggesting a new or different way does not understand there is a tradition to uphold or a pattern to complete. So, generation after generation, the family holds its sick ground, no one changing and everyone holding on to a life disconnected from truly intimate relationships.

The other break I can give is to those who were in families so sick the only way you could survive was to stake out your territory and hold on. You had a hard enough time just getting from one day to the next, and somehow you discovered something that helped you live to see another day. So rather than beat yourself up and slump down in your seat because you realize how your stubborn resistance has hurt you, feel good about the fact that at this exact moment you see it and are ready to do something about it. Find a way to be grateful because there are so many who will never see it in themselves, holding on to old destructive patterns right up through their last breath.

The Antidote to Stubborn Resistance: Willingness

If you realize this within yourself, you can be grateful because it is not easy even to see your need to change in this area. More likely than see a need to change, the stubbornly resistant person just views himself as extremely confident. Even if you get beyond the "confident" rationalization and you do see the need to change, it is very difficult to implement after you have become so ingrained in your own way of seeing the world and reacting to it defensively. Making matters even more difficult, the antidote to this problem is the exact opposite of stubborn resistance. And you can't get there in a moment or a day. It will take time. But the goal you want to reach is to have a willing heart.

Willingness is perhaps the most difficult attitude any stubbornly resistant person must develop in order to make a major life change. Willingness is a huge step on the path toward seeing your life in a whole new light. There are some simple questions to ask yourself if you are unsure whether or not you are stubbornly resistant or just confident about the way you are living your life.

Ask yourself these tough self-evaluation questions:

How frequently do I admit I was wrong?
How frequently do I ask for forgiveness?
How frequently do I ask people for their opinions?
Do I ever admit I have been approaching some problems or even my whole life in unhealthy ways?
Am I willing to admit I might need some help to move beyond the way my life is currently going?
Have I ever said: "You knew I was this way when you married me"?
Do people tell me, or do I feel I have a strong need to, always be right?
Do I stop listening to people who try to get me to see things in a different way?
Am I a "it's my way or the highway" kind of person?

These questions are just a few of the ways to consider your level of willingness. Willingness is characterized by the ability to see things from another person's perspective or at least be interested enough to acknowledge that not everyone sees things the way you do. Willing people realize not only that are they not always right, but they need to make things right when they are wrong. Willing people jump into recovery or counseling because they know there is a world of information about themselves they don't have and will not be able to find on their own. Willing people are able to shut up for a while and listen to someone else who might have something valuable to contribute to their lives. Of course the good news is that if you are even glancing through a book like this, you have a degree of willingness within you.

Life Beyond Good Intentions

One of the more subtle symptoms of stubborn willingness is a life filled with good intentions. Some people have all sorts of plans and dreams they never accomplish or experience. They are frequently telling people what they meant to do or wanted or intended to do. Over and over again, they find themselves telling people how great something would have been if they were able to pull off what they wanted. They intended to make the birthday really special. They wanted to get to that meeting. They had plans to call that counselor. They were really planning on attending that workshop. But they just could not find a way to get it done.

A person with willingness lives life beyond good intentions. There is no "try" or "want to" for the willing. The willing get things done, especially things that have lasting meaning. Willingness means that I move beyond desire to doing whatever it takes for things to be different. It is realizing that if I don't attend that meeting, I will not get feedback on my situation or problem, so I am willing to take care of every obstacle that might stand in the way of me and that meeting.

Willingness leads to change. So in thinking about where to put the good stuff in this book, I wanted to put this valuable attitude of willingness right at the front, right behind the number one roadblock of stubborn resistance.

Most likely I have told the "three men discussing their funerals" story at least one hundred times. One man says that when they are looking down at him in his coffin, he wants them to say he was a good man. The second man says he wants them to look down at the casket and say he was a good father. The third man says he wants them to look down into his casket and say, "He is moving! He is alive!" If that happened, he could get right up and take a second shot at life (with the benefit of knowing who did and did not show up at the funeral).

Of course we don't get a second chance at this life. If we live our one shot with stubborn resistance rather than willingness, we will miss much of what that life could have been, and we will die in the heap of millions who had good intentions but no real drive to be different or see things in a different light. Reframing requires willingness over stubborn resistance.

World's Largest Reframing Roadblock Number Two:
ARROGANT ENTITLEMENT

My Way

In my other life, I am a singer. Not a professional singer, but a pretty good karaoke singer. Having revealed that I sing karaoke, I know I surely must have lost a lot of respect from some readers. But it really is a lot of fun. We have taken New Life listeners on an Alaskan cruise twice. Both times I entered the ship-wide, oceanfront, sound-of-the-seas singing competition, and both times I won to the unforgettable applause of the New Life fellow travelers. The last time it was the Westerdam Superstar Competition, and I promised to change my name to Arterdam if I won. The first time I competed was on a Princess ship, and I was named Princess Idol. (I have to explain the title came from the ship and clarify I was not in a competition to become some sort of singing princess.) I won those competitions singing Frank Sinatra songs. The winning number in the first competition was one of Frank's biggest songs: "My Way."

It was a great song with strong lyrics, a catchy melody, and a huge finish. If you hit the big note at the end and hold it, there is a pretty good chance you will win. I did, and I did.

I won singing one of the most arrogant songs ever written. Perhaps it caught on because it is in the hearts of most people who hear it. We want to live our lives the way we want and then live to sing about it. For so many, life is all about doing it our very own way. Of course the Bible contradicts this with concepts like giving in to each other, not demanding our own way, and seeking out the counsel of others to determine the best way over ours. Perhaps it does not make for a very good song, but it does make for a very good life.

In the song Frank sings that he's had only a few regrets—and they're not even worth mentioning. How arrogant can you get? Not much. Everyone makes mistakes in this world. Everyone comes up short. Too much regret and you die inside or suffer emotional paralysis. Too little regret and you never evaluate where going your own way has taken you. Regret has a proper place in our lives. It humbles us to open up to the view of others, the advice of those close to us, and a perspective outside our own.

We live in a world that encourages "my way" thinking. We are bombarded with ads that tell us to "have it your way" and that "you deserve a break today." And after all, since you did not get all that you deserved in the early part of life, well, isn't it just time to go out there and get what you deserve, no matter what it does to others? And if you are not getting what you want in your work or in your relationships, doesn't that entitle you to find it wherever and however you want to? After all, isn't it really all about you and having it your way?

The Bridge to Immorality

That kind of thinking causes a conflict within most people who know what they *should* and *should not* do. They are taught to be considerate of others and care for each other and not be selfish. So for people to really tap into their entitlement, they need a bridge from what they know is right to free themselves to do what they absolutely know is not right.

Most don't just rush out to do something wrong—they inch up to it. They don't just steal at work, they convince themselves they are worth more than they make and are really just taking that to which they are entitled. They don't view it as stealing; they are just compromising a little to get what they deserve.

If in miserable marriages, they don't want to have an affair; they just know they are not satisfied. They get a little closer and closer to someone else, taking matters into their own hands, rather than trusting God for the outcome. So, fueled by their lusts and passions, they turn off their rational brains and use some very creative statements to create a bridge to what they want and are certainly entitled to.

They probably don't know it, but they are framing their actions before they ever are involved with them. They are taking some thoughts and creating a frame around the things they want to jump into. So they tell themselves:

"I deserve this."
"I have some very real special needs."
"I am in a crisis, and at least I could have this one thing."
"It really isn't betrayal because I really do still love him, and he won't ever know."
"It really isn't that bad because I know I won't go all the way."
"He really let me down, wasn't there for me, so he created this."
"I know I won't give in to temptation, so I can just flirt with this a little bit."
"Anyone in my situation would do the exact same thing."
"She felt entitled to her affair, so I am entitled to make her pay for it the rest of her life."
"I am not fully responsible because I am an addict."

If you say these things to yourself enough, you will eventually build a bridge to cross over to selfishness, and whatever you do will be framed in a way that makes it seem quite acceptable, given the circumstances.

If you do this it will start small, but this arrogant thinking will infect every area of your life, and it will destroy your relationships and the ability to heal them. It will leave you feeling dissatisfied and always wanting more, believing you deserve more than you have.

If you stay on the course of arrogant entitlement, you will always be looking for the next thing and the next person who can help you get it, and you will become a taker, a self-absorbed greedy person who uses people, takes what he can from them, and then emotionally moves on, disconnecting completely.

The Adolescent Kind of Mind

Arrogant entitlement is an adolescent state of mind. When you hit puberty, you are looking for all the things you can do. You feel entitled to new freedoms and experiences based on your age. You try to experience them with as much fun and excitement as possible. If a parent tells you that you will not be getting a new car along with the driver's license, you are amazed at the insensitivity and cruelty. If you are not allowed to view any kind of movie you deem fit to see, you are aghast at the unreasonable strictness of your parents. They restrain you in the face of all your adolescent entitlement.

Once you are into adulthood, maturity causes a change in the way you frame your options. At least it should. You stop doing anything and everything you feel entitled to, and you start doing the things you choose to be the best for you. You eliminate a lot of options just because you know they lead to destruction and more pain.

If you start eliminating things that are harmful, you may feel as if you are making great progress as a person. You see growth. But there is a long way to go. A line from the papa cow, Ben, in the movie *Barnyard* says it best: "The strong man stands up for himself. The stronger man stands up for others." With arrogant entitlement we never quite get to that next level of being concerned for others. We just stay stuck between picking things we can do that are harmful and picking things not so harmful so we can continue on the path we have chosen for ourselves. We may look less stupid because we are not getting into trouble or the hospital as often, but we are still living in a world where everything is self-focused.

Living Like Royalty

If you are living in your arrogance and demanding all you feel entitled to have, you begin to live like royalty. People start to see you that way also. But it is not good news. They see you on your throne, but you don't have much of an empire to rule. You, like the emperor with no clothes, convince yourself everything is great and your life is fantastic, but it does not appear that way to those who have a grasp on reality. To them you are "Your Royal Highness Baby" or "Sir Brat the Prince." You want what you want and you feel entitled to get it, and when you don't, you are angry, frustrated, and all about making someone else pay for your inconvenience. Every day you use people to help you get what you want. You demand and when you get what you demand, you are ungrateful. You are always looking for more than you have, believing you deserve all you can get.

You have very high expectations of what others should be doing for you. You know what you have done for them, or at least what you believe you have done for them, and you look for them to at least return the favor. You want from others what is "due" you, and you want it in a way that will please you. You have staked out your territory, you have your side of the fence, and you expect everyone to honor what you have. You think you are wise and know what you are doing, but you are living the life of the fool if you stay in your arrogant entitlement.

Proverbs 14:16 says:

> The wise are cautious and avoid danger; fools plunge ahead with great confidence.

In this careless way of life, the fool loses his close relationships as he loses himself. He does not turn from evil because he thinks he can handle it. He is blind to what he is doing and views himself as a good person. He holds himself above others as he stoops to take what he feels entitled to. It is a royal way to live: royally alone, stupid, and empty.

The Antidote to Arrogant Entitlement: Humility

It is pretty obvious what is missing from arrogantly entitled persons. They have lost or perhaps never had true humility. Humility within a person's heart eliminates the "me first," "my way," "give me what I deserve" way of thinking. Humility has no steps to climb up and over others. It reaches out to connect with others, appreciating them for who they are, not just what they can do for you. A humble person is not using everything within himself to further his own cause, but rather there is a desire to use whatever power, strength, or position to help others and meet their needs. The result is a rich life full of valuable relationships with family and friends, amassing moments of wonder where others have been helped by the efforts of a humble heart reaching out.

There are a lot of influences on us to get what we want and to believe we deserve a lot. In our world we are often left with the feeling God truly does help those who help themselves, which is often erroneously stated as a quote from the Bible. What the Bible does say is this (1 Pet. 5:6):

> So humble yourselves under the mighty power of God, and
> in his good time he will honor you.

If you live as if you believe that, you won't have need for arrogance or to reach out for what you think you are entitled to have. All you have to do is wake up each morning and start to work on your relationship with God. Start by asking for help to surrender it all to him and to humble yourself before him. Ask for the connection to grow between you and God so you are waiting on him rather than expecting others to give you what you need. This is never easy because "his good time" is likely a whole lot slower than you want. But what a life, when it is leaned up against the all-powerful God rather than leaning on everyone else!

Jesus did not just tell us to be humble, he showed us how

to humble ourselves and serve each other. One of the most profound examples of this was before the Passover and the time when Jesus would die on the cross. Knowing this torturous event was ahead, he might have felt entitled to be treated like a king and be served by his loyal followers one last time. After all, he was going to give up everything, experience the penalty of all sin, feel the agony of being removed from the presence of his Father, and endure unspeakable pain and suffering. That would certainly display enough humility and service if you ask me. But rather than seek to be served, he did the most unexpected thing: he went to his knees to humbly serve his disciples. John tells of the time in the following account:

> Jesus knew that the Father had given him authority over everything and that he had come from God and would return to God. So he got up from the table, took off his robe, wrapped a towel around his waist, and poured water into a basin. Then he began to wash the disciples' feet and to wipe them with the towel he had around him. (13:3–5)

What an example of being entitled to everything but demanding nothing. He showed us that no matter where we are or what we face, it is an opportunity to be humble before others. Rather than assert our rights, we need to give others the right-of-way. The more arrogant and entitled we feel, the more difficult that is.

The apostle Paul was a radical follower of Jesus after trying to knock off as many of Jesus' followers as he could. After living a life of dedicated service to Jesus, the way of Jesus became part of him. Paul could have complained, as many of us do, that since so much has been sacrificed for Christ, surely Christ could make the way easy for us. But Paul's life was anything but easy. He was beaten, robbed, stoned and left for dead, and imprisoned. Rather than feel he deserved better, he humbled himself and changed himself when he could not change his circumstances. In Philippians 4:11–12, he wrote:

> I have learned to be content whatever the circumstances. I know what it is to be in need, and I know what it is to have plenty. I have learned the secret of being content in any and every situation, whether well fed or hungry, whether living in plenty or in want. (NIV)

There is no way Paul could have reached that point had he held onto his arrogant entitlement. Only people who are truly humble can be content when they are needy. Humility leads to contentment and satisfaction. It spawns a life of thanksgiving rather than disappointment. Your humble heart draws people to you. They are repelled by arrogance and entitlement.

I will close this section on the world's second major roadblock to reframing with a story from a friend that sums up the difference between arrogant entitlement and humility. The story goes like this:

> A voyaging ship was wrecked during a storm at sea and only two of the men on it were able to swim to a small, desert-like island. The two survivors, not knowing what else to do, agreed they had no other recourse but prayer. However, to find out whose prayer was more powerful, they agreed to

divide the territory between them and stay on opposite sides of the island.

The first thing they prayed for was food. The next morning, the first man saw a fruit-bearing tree on his side of the land, and he was able to eat its fruit. The other man's parcel of land remained barren.

Soon the first man prayed for a house, clothes, more food. The next day, like magic, all of these were given to him. However, the second man still had nothing. Finally, the first man prayed for a ship so he could leave the island. In the morning, he found a ship docked on his side of the island. He boarded the ship and decided to leave the second man on the island.

As the ship was about to leave, the first man heard a voice from heaven booming, "Why are you leaving your companion on the island?"

"My blessings are mine alone, since I was the one who prayed for them," the first man answered. "His prayers were all unanswered, so he does not deserve anything."

"You are mistaken!" the voice rebuked him. "He had only one prayer, which I answered. If not for that, you would not have received any of my blessings."

"Tell me," the first man asked the voice, "what did he pray for that I should owe him anything?"

"He prayed that all your prayers be answered."

It is just a story, but in reality the same dynamic happens every day. We want what we want and feel entitled to have it. If we get it, we will then take into consideration what others may need. Our lives become consumed by our needs and our perspective on everything in every way.

Reframing is about seeing things from a different perspective. Why would an arrogant person want to do that? I don't think people who believe they know it all, sense it all, and have it all figured out would want to see anything but their own perspective. And they would most likely be comfortable only with people who shared their view.

Humility fixes this so you can be free to reframe the things you need to reframe. It takes practice, but it begins the next time you feel the need to step up. Just step back. It will get easier each time you try to replace arrogant entitlement with genuine humility.

World's Largest Reframing Roadblock Number Three:
JUSTIFIABLE RESENTMENT

The Most Dangerous Possession on Earth

Personal Plutonium

I doubt there are many people, certainly none in their right minds, who would be willing to walk around carrying radioactive material in their pockets. Knowing the stuff will make you sick, mutate your genes, and cause you to die a slow, painful death is enough for most everyone to avoid it at all costs. It could be considered the most dangerous possession on Earth. Dynamite or some other type of bomb would make the top-ten list. The nice thing about these materials is that they are in solid form, and when you see them you can choose to either pick them up or run from them. It is not so easy with what I believe is the most dangerous thing we can carry around inside our minds, hearts, and souls. That possession is *justifiable resentment*.

Are you angry about something in your life? Has someone hurt you, and anyone who heard about what happened would tell you that you have every right to remain angry and bitter at that person? Have you done something so awful that it will be hard ever to forgive yourself? In other words, is there something in the past you did or that was done to you, something you feel bitterness, anger, or resentment for, something anyone looking at your situation would say you are justified to feel bad about?

Perhaps you have buried it so deep or covered it so effectively you no longer recognize it is there. But when you stop and consider your life, you realize you have continued to harbor this hard place in your heart, and you believe anyone who knew about it or went through it would feel the same way. If it is there, it is as dangerous as any radioactive or explosive material that could destroy your body—only this takes who you are at the deepest levels away from you.

Petty Resentments

What I am addressing here are not all the little things we resent and get upset about on a day-to-day basis. All of us have quirky things we don't like about our situations or someone living in it with us. The other day, my wife, Misty, and I, along with our four kids, were driving down the road together when Madeline said that in driver's training they learned an acronym to help them remember what to do when they need to change lanes: SMOG. *S* stands for turn on your signal, *M* stands for look into your mirror, *O* stands for look over your shoulder, and *G* stands for hit the gas and make the turn. I said I tend to use the GAS method: *G* stands for gun it, *A* stands for ask everybody in the car if they see anything in the way, and S stands for slam on the brakes right before I hit anyone.

Well, when I admitted my method, Misty started laughing and could not stop for at least five minutes—and then she would crank it up again every time the thought came back to her. Why? Because I had so accurately nailed the driving technique that causes her so much irritation and anguish.

My wife cannot stand the way I drive anything. Whether it's in the car, a boat, or a lawn mower, how I drive seems to drive her up the wall. I have come to realize that older men allow women to drive not because they are old but to stay sane. So you will often see her driving me around just to avoid the conflict that comes when I brake too slowly, drive too fast, or cruise too close to the curb.

These are just petty resentments—her of my driving, me of her hating my driving. We all have these, and the more of them we give up, the better we feel about each other. They are not going to kill us if we see them as part of everyday life and everyone's being human.

If my wife were to say to someone she is miserable and full of agony and doesn't know where to turn because of my driving, not many would say they totally understand why her whole life is ruined because of my driving. Only someone with terminal codependency would give her the feeling she is entitled to go through life focused on my not using my turn signal enough or not caring that the person I just cut off may be scarred for life. If my driving went from irritation to an irrational, deep-seated source of resentment, no one would affirm her in that. We all have these types of irritations with each other that hopefully remain just that: minor irritations we learn to live with.

Roots of Bitterness

The expression "learn to live with" means we adjust to or accommodate the humanity of another and learn to accept it as part of the reality of being imperfect people. But there is another "learn to live with" that actually is more about learning to die. It deals with a hurt or a wound that goes so deep it implants in our hearts a *root of bitterness*. I love this phrase because it so accurately describes the source of so much of our misery: not a limb lopped off or a trunk chopped down, but a root that must be dug out of the ground of our pasts and destroyed forever.

The Bible addresses this heart problem directly in Ephesians 4:31, where we are told to "get rid of all bitterness, rage, [and] anger." We are not instructed to get rid of all bitterness *unless* someone has done something really horrible to us. We are not instructed to verify what happened as so horrible that we are justified in our resentment. No, we are told clearly to get rid of all of it.

Why? Because it eats away at us, redirects our lives, takes away our drive to fulfill our purposes in life, and taints all our relationships. It also dishonors God, who has forgiven us of so much and wants us to be willing to forgive others. Job 5:2 reveals that "resentment destroys the fool," and we see it happen all the time. We either chain ourselves to a past or a person we cannot change who produced pain we cannot undo, or we find a way to move on, give up our right to resent, and even one day find a way to forgive.

The Antidote to Justifiable Resentment: Forgiveness

Forgiving Without Limits

Without exception we are to forgive, no matter how justified we feel due to the severity of the offense. When Peter wanted to clarify the concept of forgiveness with Jesus, he was thinking that seven times was the limit. But in Matthew 18:22, Jesus came up with a calculation of seventy times seven, indicating that the number of times we need to forgive is unlimited. We have a mandate to forgive. Often we look for any loophole possible to withhold forgiveness, but there is none. We must forgive.

I have had times when I thought it was just too much to ask me to forgive. In one instance a businessman literally took from me more than one million dollars in cancelled contracts and unfulfilled commitments. I am not exaggerating what this "Christian" businessman did to me, all the while acting like he was full of love and compassion. In another instance, a person in ministry did not take any money from me, but she betrayed me after convincing me she could be trusted. And then there was an instance where I uncovered infidelity. In all three of these situations I was astounded at the deep pain that felt unbearable, and I could not believe, on top of it all, that I had to forgive these people. From the second I was hurt by each of them, I was aware of the task at hand: the need to forgive, even though anyone who knew the situations closely would see I was entitled to any amount of anger, rage, resentment, or bitterness. Well, I felt all that, but I very quickly began to let go of it. I knew the longer I held on to it, the more I would be hurt by it.

The forgiveness was not instant. It took time. I had to work through the pain I felt. I had to work through all the wounds from my childhood these betrayals tapped into. I had to look at my own sinful nature and ability to mess up, and I had to slowly but surely move on with my life. I knew if I held on to unforgiveness, I could derail my life forever. I have always pushed ahead and kept going. That was what my father taught me to do: Keep going. Take initiative and be responsible. I knew the longer I wallowed in anger and bitterness, the more vulnerable I was to derailing my life into something I was not meant to do or be.

So I forgave in each case. I forgave and I let God be the avenger if any revenge was appropriate. As I write this, I have no malice in my heart for any of these people. I am free.

To be free from the negative influence of these people and what they did to me, or as some would say, all the things I allowed them to do, I had to do the work I am recommending you do. I had to reframe them using material sent from God: His truth. His grace for me and for them. His demand for me to forgive. My awareness of all he forgave of me.

His hope led me to believe no matter what anyone did to me or took away from me, he would restore it. I had hope that even the worst pain could be transformed into something of value in my life. So I reframed these people as tools of God, imperfect tools God was using to transform my character.

Since I personally needed so much work, I did not really have the time or energy to continue to focus on all of their faults. Gradually I came to see them as no worse than I and even better in some ways. I could then move on with my life.

Once I reframed these people and what they did, I was ready to resolve it. I did that by grieving what I lost, working through the fear of what might lie ahead of me, experiencing the pain and letting go of its source. I began to heal. And key to all that healing were the supportive people I had standing by me.

The reframing and the resolution took about the same amount of time. But the next phase took even longer.

Eventually I was able to move on and refocus my life away from the tragedy of events. I began to look at the tragedies of others who had been hurt, and I wanted to help them. My biggest embarrassment gave me an open door into the hearts of those who had been through the same betrayals. They were drawn to me, and I had a deeper connection to them than ever.

Refocusing on them at the right time was the completion of my healing, allowing me to feel that none of my pain was wasted. God was and would use it to help others who were struggling and bumbling as I had. But it all began with reframing reality. If I had not known to start there, I might have remained stuck in my misery and in a past I could not alter.

The worst place my life might have gotten stuck was in this area of forgiveness. If I had not known I needed to forgive, and if I had framed forgiveness as something I was giving to someone who did not deserve it rather than a passage to my own freedom, I might never have made it out of my past. I needed to reframe, and I needed to forgive most of all.

The Process

When we forgive, it is a process rather than an event. Some have been hurt so badly, they would need five years to get over their wounds. For others it could take even longer. If that is the case for you, it is best to start now with the process. That beginning might be nothing more than the realization you are holding on to something from the past and you feel justified in your feelings about it. But those negative feelings are not doing anything to the people who hurt you—except allowing them to continue to negatively impact your life. You are letting them dominate your life. It is time to acknowledge they have remained the focus of too much time and attention, and now that you see it, you will begin to let it go.

I don't know of anything that keeps a person from the reframing process more than this feeling of justifiable resentment. It is such a cancer on the soul. The bitterness is within you, not the person who hurt you. Your anger may give you a sense of power, but it actually robs you of your power, drains off your potential, and poisons all your relationships. That is why, for your sake, not the sake of the offender, you must begin the healing and forgiving process. It is just a beginning, but it is one step away from a bitter and wasted life focused on the past rather than enjoying the present and preparing for the future.

One of the most beautiful promises in Scripture is found in Matthew 11:28–30. These are the words of Jesus inviting us to a different way of living than the world offers.

Come to me, all you who are weary and burdened, and I will give you rest. Take my yoke upon you and learn from me, for I am gentle and humble in heart, and you will find rest for your souls. For my yoke is easy and my burden is light. (NIV)

He invites us to come closer to him because he wants to give us something we need. He wants to give us rest. He wants to teach us his gentle and humble ways, which will bring peace to our souls. His way is so much easier and lighter than our own. And his way, his life, is all about forgiveness.

As long as we foster bitterness and harbor resentment, we will damage our ability to reframe and move on with our lives. This is not just a roadblock to reframing, it is a roadblock to living. So at some point, and hopefully that point is now, you have to courageously move toward giving up your resentment and begin replacing it with forgiveness, especially when the forgiveness is not deserved.

I go back to 1 Peter 4:1 and remind myself that it is when I am ready to suffer that I am ready to stop sinning. Anything, like a grudge, that causes me to fall short of the mark is sin. So I can either suffer in my sin, or I can suffer in getting out of it and learning to forgive. When I endure suffering to get out of sin, I have already begun to reframe my life. I have moved away from my feelings' being in control to allowing dominion to God's truth in my life.

World's Largest Reframing Roadblock Number Four:
DISCONNECTED ISOLATION

The Perfection of Disconnection

I don't have any problems relating to people. Really. It's true. I have no problems with being who I am, I don't ever get irritated or upset with anyone—*as long as I am alone.* It is when I gather with others that I have to come face-to-face with who I am. The worst in me can lie dormant for years as long as no one is around to awaken the sleeping giant. It is amazing just how easy life is when I am isolated. You would really like me if you observed me alone.

But the "perfection" that many of us experience when we are alone and disconnected is flawed. Life is easier for us, but it is emptier. We don't have to face who we really are so we don't know the areas in which we need to grow. Stagnation becomes comfortable and we stop developing the maturity and wisdom God wants for us.

If I have no one to challenge me, I can remain in complete denial. I can do what I want and never have to question whether or not it is the right or best thing for me. I can feed all my bad habits and deep resentments and allow them to shrink my life and potential. I can take my place alongside the millions of others who have decided to surrender to a life with the least resistance and least chance for meaning and purpose.

For those who have settled into this rut, it seems like the perfect way to live. Some are so ingrained they view it as the way life was meant to be. In reality, it is the perfect setup to *miss* life as it is meant to be.

The Disconnected Life

This roadblock to reframing is a tough one to counter. People who have developed disconnected lives rarely see the need to reframe anything. They have made their assessment that the world is unsafe, people are not worth the trouble, or they are inadequate for any type of relationship. They accept these beliefs as if they were irrefutable facts and live their lives accordingly.

They don't want to be bothered with seeing things from a different perspective. They have made up their minds about themselves, people, and life in general and prefer not to be confused by someone suggesting they may not be exactly on target.

I know this because I spent much of my life with this mind-set. I came from a very stubborn family that did not want to be told there was a different or better way. This stubbornness hurt us in many areas, as we lived with a certain arrogance that we had the answers many others did not have. My grandfather was the most hardheaded man I have ever known. I admired his unwaivering confidence, but it often got in the way of anything he was involved with. And I have found myself living in his hand-me-down genes many times.

Right now I am looking out at the lake where we live. My grandfather lived on a lake, and it has been in my blood since I was a child. I am just now fulfilling a dream I have had of living on a lake as he did. But his house on the lake was a bit different from ours.

My grandfather built his lake house with his five sons. Just the fact that they knew how to do that amazes me. They built a small cabin on the lake with a huge porch that could sleep about twenty people. Some of my best memories were generated in that handcrafted home. The family, with five sons and about eighty grandkids and great grandkids, outgrew the little cabin, so they added on. And they did it all themselves.

It turned out to be a nice place, more than doubling the size of the original cabin, but it had one major flaw. My grandfather had not calculated into the ceiling height the fact that the new addition had a foundation about twelve inches higher than that of the original cabin. So the ceiling in the new area was a foot shorter than it was supposed to be. If you were not looking, you could walk right into the ceiling fan and permanently injure yourself. You felt as if you needed to hunch over when you were in the big room. And it was all because my stubborn grandfather would not listen to his boys, who told him from the beginning that something was very wrong with the plans.

I came by my disconnection tendencies honestly through the bloodlines of my parents. And just like my heritage, I can be in a crowd of many and still be isolated and disconnected. It was all I knew from very early on. It was modeled by my father and mother and my older brothers. I took up where they left off and lived as if relationships were optional in life, something you could take care of after everything else was completed. I lived inside my head.

If you live in yours, you have no difficulty understanding the concept. You live alone inside your head, bumping into people every now and then, but there is no deep connection to anyone. My internal isolation seemed like the perfect place to live, and it was not easy to see that I had gotten it all wrong. My world needed reframing, and it was hard to see it needed an overhaul with no one close enough to speak to my heart in a way I would hear. It took a lot of pain before I was able to wake up to a different and better way.

The Antidote to Perfect Disconnection: Intimacy

Imperfect Intimacy

In the intimate relationships of life, we open our hearts and minds to a new way of looking at reality. We open up to another person's point of view. We become vulnerable enough to look at how we are making mistakes as we imperfectly relate to people who care for and reveal themselves deeply to us. We see our own flaws in this type of relationship. We feel the need for a lot of minor and some major adjustments in relationships that are growing more and more intimate. After living with perfect disconnection, we do not realize this quickly or easily. It takes time.

One of the difficult things about intimacy is that if we have been hurt in the past, it is the opposite of what we think we need and want. We think our greatest need is protection to prevent any further damage. But it is not protection we need, it is safe connection to help us view the world in a different way.

Who can blame a person who was abused early in life for defining all relationships according to that abuse? Who could blame someone who was abandoned emotionally or even physically for believing that all relationships end up in abandonment? It would be only natural to hunker down and protect oneself after being so cruelly treated as a child. From that stance the world and people would seem very unsafe.

That view would be hard to give up. But it is in reframing our current relationships that we come to experience great lives. So the beginning of a reframed life is making the move to connect in deeper and more intimate ways with others. It does not fix everything, but it is a giant step toward seeing life as it really is.

Your Right Versus What Is Right

If you have grown up not knowing how to develop intimate relationships because no one taught you, then you can blame your isolation on some weirdo parents who just never gave it to you. In fact, what they might have taught you was how to perfectly destroy intimate relationships and that is what you have modeled. Whether it is just stepping back and withdrawing or stepping up and attacking, you learned a crummy way of relating from them and it gives you the perfect right to continue relating that way.

But at some point you may want to give up that right in order to find what is beneficial in building a life reframed by healthy relationships. You may want to learn to grow closer to God and others and enjoy a fulfilling life in close proximity to them. You will no longer need to "run for the hills" emotionally or mentally to feel safe.

Sadly, it is not just our experience from childhood that can frame our lives in a disconnected and isolated manner. Sometimes it can come from religious teaching. I don't say it comes from Christian teaching, because true Christian teaching follows the example of Christ. Christ did not live in isolation. He connected with the outcasts, the lowly, and the unlikely. He had a group of men around him he loved and accepted with all their flaws. He taught how to be in relationship. So isolative thinking that prevents reframing does not come from Christ.

But there are religious teachings that are spoken in the name of Christ that lead to isolation. None of those teachings is more powerful than when the word *submission* is addressed.

Taken out of context, submission is taught as something women should do to men. It puts men in a one-up position and entitles them to trample on women and treat them as "less than." So this teaching has produced many marriages where men are totally isolated on top of the relationship and women are walled off down below, prohibited from connecting and experiencing fulfilling relationships with others.

Dictator-Doormat Theology

Most of this teaching starts and stops with one verse, Ephesians 5:22, which reads:

> You wives will submit to your husbands as you do to the Lord.

That sounds pretty clear-cut if you just walk around with that one verse in your head. It is a license to kill every marital opportunity for intimate connection. It enables a man to live in perfect disconnection as a dictator, trampling over his doormat wife, and all in the name of Scripture.

But anyone taking that course is using truth in an untruthful way. Let me repeat that: it is possible to take the truth of the Bible and use it in an untruthful way, and this is perhaps exhibit A in crimes against people in the name of God. And it is all because men take it out of context and use it to avoid self-examination and to keep their wives "in their place."

All you have to do is back up one verse and you get the proper context in which Paul gave the command. Ephesians 5:21 reads:

> And further, you will submit to one another out of reverence for Christ.

The concept being taught here is a *mutual submission* that builds connection.

Then after looking at the context and the concept, there is a principle of wives submitting to husbands, which lends itself to connection. Think of the opposite of wives submitting to husbands—I see that all the time. They go off and do what they want, rebel against the husband and family responsibility, and enter into other relationships that betray everything right and good about marriage. Wives submitting to husbands is a good thing in the context of submitting to one another under the concept of mutual submission. But wives submitting is just the first part of making that concept happen.

From Mutuality to Intimacy

The second part is found a few verses later in Ephesians 5:25. Now if you stop at the verse 22, you never get to see the other part of the context and concept. But the command is just as clear for the man and just as radical as submitting is for the woman. Ephesians 5:25 reads:

And you husbands must love your wives with the same love
Christ showed the church. He gave up his life for her.

If you ask me, that sure puts the kibosh on the dictator-
doormat arrangement and invites both spouses to reframe their
entire concept of marriage. If verse 25 doesn't, the final verse
in the entire passage restates the obvious and powerfully tells
each partner the proper frame in which intimacy can grow.
Ephesians 5:33 reads:

So again I say, each man must love his wife as he loves himself, and the wife must respect her husband.

Throughout this passage Paul describes a mutuality that
builds connection and intimacy.

I have spent so much time on this because if there is no
mutuality in a relationship, there is no intimacy. Additionally,
this book is about reframing and taking a second look at the way
we have viewed things over time. The men who cling to this
dictator-doormat concept of one-way submission tend to have
a very difficult time in looking at things in a new light because
they are so highly entrenched and invested in their views. If
you or someone you love is like this, perhaps the best book on
reframing your view of the marital relationship is *Every Man's
Marriage*. My name is on the book as coauthor, but it is Fred
and Brenda Stoeker's story of how they reframed their marriage.
More importantly, it is the story of how Fred reframed his view
of marriage, his wife, and all women.

I will close this section with three verses, and the first one
is from 1 John 2:10. It reads:

Anyone who loves other Christians is living in the light and does not cause anyone to stumble.

A married man or woman living in the same house but living alone and isolated is causing the other to stumble. Rather than withdraw into a solitary life of disconnected isolation, do what you can to rebuild the bridge back to the other's heart. And if you are single, make sure you are single for some other reason than a fear of vulnerability. We are looking at anything that may be keeping you stuck in old patterns of a lifestyle that is not getting you where you want to go.

Finally, two more very self-evident truths from Romans 14:19 and then Ephesians 4:2:

Let us therefore make every effort to do what leads to peace and to mutual edification. (NIV)

Be completely humble and gentle; be patient, bearing with one another in love. (NIV)

World's Largest Reframing Roadblock Number Five:
BLIND IGNORANCE

This book is all about countering blind ignorance. I am approaching the concept of reframing from many different angles hoping that one will pierce your defenses and motivate you to make some changes. Just the fact that you are this far into the book says you want to be informed, you want to know the truth and how to apply it to your life. Sometimes we don't have the knowledge to make the best choices. We are doing the best we can, but we lack information to turn things around. Often people will go to a seminar and expect some emotional experience that will change everything, but people are usually changed by a new way of viewing life or framing it in a different way.

Take Off the Blinders

So often we are ignorant of our own condition. We don't fully grasp the reality of our lives because we have no one willing to tell us the truth about ourselves, and we tend to distort the truth we see so we don't have to go through some uncomfortable changes. We are all blind in some ways and the only way we will see reality is if we are willing to take the blinders off, allow others to speak truth to us, and allow God's Word to seep truth into our lives.

In Isaiah 43:8 the prophet addressed people of his day, but he could just as easily have been talking to us. He said:

Bring out the people who are blind,
even though they may have eyes,
And the deaf, even though they have ears. (NASB)

People then (and people now) were missing the reality of their lives, not able to see what was really going on and not able to hear those who were trying to challenge their way of thinking to help them. When we are caught up in our own world, seeing things the way we want to see them, it is hard to see ourselves and our own problems.

I love the tale of the elderly man and his wife who walked

into a fine art gallery. This man had once served on the board and knew quite a bit about fine art. As they entered the lobby, he looked at the image hanging there and, in his arrogant and grouchy manner, began to critique it. He said, "First of all, that frame is not even fit for a fine painting. It has no place in an art gallery. Second, the subject is not worthy to be in a painting. He is lifeless, drab, and there is no meaning to the painting." His wife interrupted, "Honey, that is not a painting. That is a mirror."

It is difficult to see the reality of our lives. We need people and truth to mirror who we are and what we need to do to get on with our lives. You will feel no need to reframe your life if you never see it for what it really is.

The Antidote to Blind Ignorance: Obedience

You can't just read God's Word to know how to live your life; you have to do what it tells you to do so you can know God's will. John 8:31–32 tells us if we follow the teachings of Christ, we are proving we are his disciples. If we do that, we will then come to know the truth. Truth will become part of us and will set us free. So the antidote to living in blind ignorance, where you can't frame your life because you don't see a need to do so, is living out the truth from God's Word.

You read it and incorporate it into your life. You read it and obey it. You read it and respond to it by doing the next right thing. You read it and it becomes a new way of thinking, a new way of framing all you do. It also reframes how you feel about yourself and your future.

Roadblocks Summary

If you want to benefit from the rest of this book, you have to sacrifice some things that have become very dear to you. You have to release your stubborn resistance, let go of your arrogant entitlement, put away your justifiable resentments, come out of your perfect disconnection, and refuse to live in blind ignorance.

Allow your life to fill up with things that can help you reframe the most difficult aspects of your life. Become willing to try a new way to live. Humble yourself before others so you can exist on a level plane with everyone else. Begin the process of forgiveness by trying to understand a bit about the lives of those who have hurt you. Connect mutually with those you love so you can experience deeper intimacy in relationships.

And finally, read God's Word, learn it, and live it so you can be set free by it. Changing from the old patterns to these healthy new ones opens the door to reframing all areas of your life.

CHAPTER THREE

Who Benefits
from Reframing?

Past Hurt: Present Pain

There are those who seem so strong and skilled that they appear able to do anything. Perhaps they have climbed to the top of a tough and demanding corporation. Or they have done a great job of raising some very difficult kids in the worst of circumstances. Looking at the outside, we see they seem to conquer whatever is in their way.

Then we look a little deeper and find they are holding on to something that impacted their lives in a horrific way. Something that happened years ago still impacts the lives they live today. And it does so in a way that seems as if it just happened yesterday.

These are people who can be helped by reframing because the lack of forgiveness could simply be a result of their not ever getting started. And they may never have started because they could not see the person who hurt them as deserving of forgiveness.

I remember talking to a woman who wanted to know the best way to get someone to ask for her forgiveness. I thought that was an unusual question. Most people would ask how to move past being hurt by someone who has never asked for forgiveness, but that was not what she wanted. She wanted the person to come to her, admit he was wrong, and ask to be forgiven. I very quickly assumed there must have been some minor spat that occurred with someone close to her, and she wanted an apology so they could get on with the relationship. But that was not the case at all.

She revealed she had married a man about thirty years before and he divorced her after falling in love with a woman from work whom he later married. The divorce had occurred more than twenty years prior. And now, years later, she didn't date much. She wanted her ex-husband to be remorseful enough to ask for her forgiveness after twenty years.

This is a classic example of someone safely stuck in a past hurt. The wasted opportunities and emotion were incalculable. She did not seem to grasp how unusual it would be for her to still want and need an apology from someone who had not been in her life for such a long time.

As we spoke more, I discovered one of the deepest hurts from her childhood came when her father divorced her mother to marry someone else, leaving her feeling very uncared for and unloved. Her husband knew of this deep wound. He knew how hard it had been for her ever to trust any man again. He knew her heart had been broken badly, and the one thing she asked of him was to not marry her until he knew beyond a shadow of a doubt he could be faithful to her for a lifetime. That he knew this deep wound and then betray her after she had been so cautious was more than she could bear. It was the unforgivable sin she thought no one would ever commit against her.

Holding on to a Meaningless Hope

Once the betrayal happened, she shut down her emotional life and just focused on him and what he took from her. During the divorce she fought for every penny her lawyer could get out of him. Then she refused to get on with her life. She was waiting for his life to crash and burn and him to come crawling back.

Well, it did not crash and burn. His second marriage stayed intact, and she finally had to face the reality that he was not ever coming back to her. With that possibility out of the picture, she held on to one thing, and it was an apology and a request for forgiveness. So she wanted to know the best way to make something like that happen.

Reframing can help people who are living in present pain due to a past hurt. This woman needed to reframe her dilemma from one of not having an apology from him to one of not being willing to move on with her life. She needed to see that in the beginning the blame, if she wanted to blame, for the affair could be placed on him. But now the problem was not the husband's affair or the divorce. The problem was hers. She had to take the focus off what he did and put the focus on her response to what he did.

If she did not do that, she would remain stuck for her remaining years. But she had twenty or thirty good years left, and I certainly did not want her to waste those wishing for something that would never happen and use that as an excuse to close down her life rather than open it up to new possibilities.

Exploring the Reframing Options

This woman also needed to reframe this man from one who was all bad to one who made a bad choice. The fact that his second marriage lasted showed that he was not all bad. He had hurt her in a horrible way, but he did not spend all of his life hurting others. Perhaps he learned from his mistake. Perhaps once he was married, he wished he had never victimized her. There was also the possibility he felt he could never live up to her expectations and in a strange way freed her to go and find someone who could. She also needed to reframe the perspective that he lived in regret and shame over betraying her.

There were many different ways she could reframe what happened so long ago and what that meant to her life today. And until she pulled her head out of her hurt to take a second look at how she was staying stuck, she probably would not be able to forgive and move on. Reframing would not fix her problem, but it could begin the process of getting her unstuck from a past she could not change.

An Invitation to Anyone Stuck

Anyone who is stuck in the past and cannot find a way to forgive someone can benefit from reframing. Looking at the options allows you to take a step back and see the other person and your life since the offense in the proper perspective.

The goal is to remove the influence of the abuser or the one who abandoned as soon as possible.

Forgiveness can seem to be just too much to ask. So reframing can help by helping yourself to see it all in a whole new light. Your choice is either to reframe or to continue to wait for something that most likely will never happen.

In situations like this, some are unwilling to forgive the persons who hurt them. They believe the abusers deserve the worst, and they think forgiving the perpetrators lets them off the hook. Others just cannot get over the pain they went through. They continue to relive that pain and are often defined by it. When they let go, they regain their ability to live healthily in the present and develop lives with purpose for the future.

I have also seen those who were unable to live beyond a horrific event. Some World War II veterans I have met in alcohol and drug treatment centers don't have a grasp of much of anything other than the hardships they suffered in the war. Their lives today revolve around that time, talking about it and reliving it. Reframing that horrible time could help the veterans see the war as part of their lives rather than all of their lives. This disabling focus on past events probably was more common among Vietnam veterans, who not only endured terrible hardships but often felt it was a worthless sacrifice or that they did not get the proper respect due them.

Seeing the "Benefits" of Living in the Past

When people are so stuck in the past, they actually discover some benefits that are hard to let go of. They see their lives as permanently tainted by the event. In reframing they become able to see what they have done *to themselves* in response to the original trauma. One "benefit" is that they don't have to fully participate in life because they are "damaged goods." Another "benefit" is if they are focused on the past, they don't have to take the risks involved in new relationships—relationships that might not turn out so well.

Perhaps the most common "benefit" of not moving on is that it becomes the excuse for everything done in excess. It is the excuse for overeating, overdrinking, overspending, or over-anything. People believe that all of this overindulgence is a result of this sad thing in the past. So those who were hurt "benefit" in a sick way, justifying hurting themselves and "benefiting" by not having to look at the source of the excessive behavior.

Assistance for the Disconnected

Reframing can benefit those who are unable to connect deeply with others. It can help them see how they are setting themselves up for rejection or how their overly self-protective lifestyle is harming them. If they can reframe it, they may be able to repair the problem. Otherwise they will find themselves rejected and abandoned again.

Five years ago I worked with a woman who joined a Bible study with some very affluent other women. They welcomed her, and she was excited to be in the group. Some in the group were celebrities and others were extremely wise as well as well-off materially.

But within four weeks the group failed to include her in some events. Then they asked her to not come back to the meeting.

In reframing that whole episode, she was able to see some details she had overlooked. In the beginning she framed it all from the perspective of her needs, her rights, and her mistreatment by these "coldhearted" women. But these women had been offended by some of the things she did. They were even more offended when they talked to her about them, and she did not take them seriously. They asked her to come on time, and she never did. It was a disruption they were not willing to tolerate. After she didn't bring her Bible, they requested she do so, and she brought one the size of Texas, seemingly to mock their request. They did not like the way she spoke of her husband in negative terms. Everything was his fault and everything about their marriage was his problem, and the negativity was infecting everything they discussed. So they went to her, asked her to look at what she was doing, and when she acted as if she did not care, they asked her to leave.

The reframing helped her to see there were patterns in her life she was blind to. These women had done her a favor in asking her to change some things others were too afraid to discuss. She needed to reframe them as reasonable and reframe herself as the demanding, inconsiderate person who had lost touch with the feelings of others. She had become the center of attention, and all that mattered to her was how she felt or how she was perceived, and if these women had not confronted her, she might have gone her whole life offending people, using them to make herself feel good and rejecting them whenever they did anything but boost her ego.

The reframing she needed to do led to her making major life changes. Had she continued to see things only in the light of her own perspective, she would have never been able to grow beyond her own self-obsession.

The Disconnectors

Several things commonly cause disconnection from others. Anyone who struggles with making or keeping a connection can benefit from looking at these disconnectors and evaluate if reframing their relationships might eliminate some of these.

One of the biggest is not being able to connect with another person's pain. It can stem from an internal focus on your own pain or a disregard for the other person's value. But once people sense that you are not sensitive to the reality of their pain, they most likely will not want to continue or deepen the relationship. You can get so caught up in your own wound you no longer care about the wounds of someone else. You can even go to the extreme of evaluating others soley based on how they respond to your wound. What you cannot or will not do for them, you demand from them when it comes to your own personal pain and wounds.

The other big disconnector may be your being so deeply ingrained in your painful past so that you are unable to endure the pain of someone else. You resist getting into their lives because you are afraid it may cause you to break under the load of so much agony. When others sense, in their darkest hour, you are only protecting your own heart, they walk away to find someone who will care.

Additionally, if you are in so much pain all the time, you may have a neediness that drives others away. They cannot meet the demands you put on a relationship, so they reject you. Reframing can help a person in this situation see the problem from a different perspective. The rejected can come to see themselves as contributors to the problem rather than solely as victims of others hurting them.

Conflict, Confusion, and Complications

Reframing can benefit those whose relationships are riddled with conflict, confusion, and complications. We relate in the ways we have been taught or the ways modeled to us. Some of that teaching and modeling have not been too healthy. But often we are repeating the same problems because it is all we know. We are convinced this is how relationships are supposed to work.

If we are willing to go through some reframing of our problems with others, we may discover that we lack an understanding of our role in a relationship. We may think it is our role to lead when it would be a better stance to cooperate. We may think we are not entitled to express our desires, so we cease to be real in the relationship, and the other person has difficulty respecting us or even knowing who we really are. If we reframe what we are doing, we may find we are too dominant or too passive, too demanding or too subservient, too protective or too revealing. Reframing helps in seeing how the roles we take may produce results we don't want.

There are other ways we kill relationships. I have seen so many people who want connection and relationship experience repeated rejection and have no idea why. They appear to be the perfect candidates for relationship. They love the connection. They want to be vulnerable, and they love hearing their partners share intimate details and struggles. But in all of this desire for connection and attachment, they fail to see what is actually happening in the relationship. If they could reframe the relationship and their role in it, they would see the problem is their neediness. They have unrealistic needs that no one could meet. Yet, that is all they are looking for: someone to meet those unrealistic needs. What seem to be attempts at connection are actually a form of begging—begging to get what cannot be fulfilled by one person.

When needy persons get involved with reframing, they can start to see their unrealistic demands and their bottomless pit of expectations. They can also come to see some of the realistic needs of other people. Expectations of others become more realistic and authentic, rather than needy ways of connecting. Meeting the needs of others rather than desperately trying to find any way to hang onto or control them becomes a point of strong connection. Reframing allows the needy person to see what is unhealthy attachment and what produces pseudo-intimacy. Relationships can be built on mutual respect and authentic desire rather than be dominated by fear, shame, control, and desperation.

From Potential to Productivity

I discovered a weird thing about myself. While I have great compassion for people who are hurting and struggling, I am often the most bothered by those who have not conquered something I have. I know you might be thinking I should go back and read what I wrote about arrogance, and I think arrogance is part of this phenomenon. But I have seen it in so many others as well.

For instance, I used to smoke, and I know how difficult it is to quit. I know the struggle of finally feeling free from the most addictive chemical on the market and then to experience the frustration of being lured so easily right back into it. No one knows that agony better than I, but I think I am less tolerant of those who smoke than those who never have.

You would think it would be just the opposite. But other ex-smokers I have been with have been the first to speak up when there is stray smoke in the room. They seem defiant and bent on eradicating smoking from the planet while the "never smoked" don't seem fazed by it.

I said all that to try to ease into this next category that needs reframing. It is the category of the unmotivated underachiever. If you find yourself in that category, I know reframing can help you because I have been where you are and know how difficult it is to get out of that rut. (But I probably have way too little tolerance for this type of existence.)

When I was in this place in my life, the word that most offended me was always meant as a compliment—it was the word *potential*. I hated having potential. To me it just meant all the gifts and strengths I had got me nowhere because they were underutilized. Who in the world wants to have on his tombstone: "Here Lies a Person Who Had Great Potential"? People with great potential are frustrated people whose dreams have not come true. Reframing could be the thing that moves them a step up out of mere potential to a lifestyle of productivity.

If you are following in my footsteps, or more accurately my "butt impressions" on the couch where I ate, watched television, talked on the phone, read the first few pages of hundreds of books, looked through hundreds of mail-order catalogues, and wished for the days when I could find my niche in life, then you probably have run into some of the following obstacles:

- You know and feel and hate that you are achieving so below your abilities.
- You have severe difficulties with being distracted.

- You find it hard to consistently stay focused on the priority at hand.
- You get involved with things with intensity and excitement but those are quickly followed by boredom and disinterest.
- You find yourself putting a lot of energy into things that require a lot of time but produce very few important results.

If this is you, reframing can help you get off the couch and get on with your life. All people have their own view or frame of reality keeping them stuck in a nonachievement mode. It is a belief if adhered to forever, will result in the tombstone I described. But if you give up that one little belief (or perhaps several you have collected), you are able to see the world in a totally different way. Then you can make your way off the couch and out into the world.

My false belief was that life would all work out and I did not need to know where I was headed. I had no idea what I really wanted to do. I knew what would show more responsibility, but it wasn't something I wanted to do. So I just drifted in and out of college without doing much studying, refusing to take on anything that was a challenge. If something like German turned out to be a bit tougher than anticipated, I just dropped it and continued to think I would make my way to what I wanted to do.

Over and over I have seen lazy, nonproductive people stubbornly live with this view of the world. They take pride in making it part of their identity. They will say things like

"I don't really like to have a plan that might get messed up."
"Who wants to always be disappointed because something you decided to do, you can't do?"

"Let's just figure out what we want to do once we get
    started."
"I don't think money is that important and if I have not
    saved enough now, I can make up for it later."

And on and on you go, using excuses not to accomplish
much of anything worthwhile.

There are a lot of reasons for these false beliefs that can
be reframed. Some are perfectionistic, so they won't do anything unless they are very sure they can do it perfectly—or
at least better than anyone else. Others have a fear of being
overwhelmed, so they just don't attempt anything unless it is
easy. And underlying so much of this type of thinking is a mild
depression that needs to be treated so the chemicals in the
brain can start working for you rather than against you. Finally,
some carry a feeling of failure implanted by a repeated suc-
cession of failures or a parent who drummed it into them that
they would fail.

Whatever the source, reframing can help the person who
needs to get busy doing the things that matter the most and
leave behind those things that don't matter at all.

Reframing the Largest Most Valuable and Powerful Number in the World

If you are on hold and your life reeks with stagnation and inactivity, if it seems your brain may be rotting from inactivity and
your body deteriorating as it grows in size, there is one reframing device that would benefit you more than others. Not only
do you want to reframe (as in revise) the way you see the world,
but you want to reframe (as in restructure) from the inside out.

If you will do this, it can have dramatic results in multiple areas of your life. And it involves the largest, most challenging but most valuable and powerful number in the world. That number is *one*. The power of one can reframe your mind from the inside and reframe how you view everything you see on the outside.

The first thing I suggest for anyone who has a hard time getting things accomplished—you have stacks of items you need to go through, people you need to call, and chores you need to get done—is to begin to implant a big fat number one firmly in your head. If I were you, I would go to a school supply store where they sell numbers or buy some construction paper and cut out some big bold number ones. Then I would place them wherever I find myself hanging out. I would picture that number in as many ways and colors as I possibly could so my mind, which was at one time blank, was now full of the number one all over the place.

Every structure of your mind is reframed with number one. You focus on that number so much you start to ask about anything that happens, how it relates to the number one. One becomes a word, a symbol, and a figure that you saturate your mind with inside and out. Even when you are driving the car, reading a magazine, or watching television, you are looking for that number so it becomes part of the framework inside your brain.

I know it sounds a bit silly, but if you are looking for a way out of a rut, this is a path that can take you where you want to go. All you are doing is increasing your awareness of where everything worth anything starts. It all starts with the number one.

The Power of One

The power of one is found in reframing the structure of your mind to focus on what you have the ability to do and move out of thinking on what is too much for you to do. It is trading in the impossible and unattainable for what is completely within your grasp. After years of living convinced of what cannot be done, it is not easy to break out and become productive. That is why restructuring with the number one is so important. The time of ruminating on that number is like hitting a reboot key for your brain over and over again. Eventually when you restart it, your brain begins to view things differently and life begins to feel different.

For a long time I wanted to write books. But I just never found the time. It was an impossibility for me to find the time to write even a one-hundred-page book. My much too easily distracted mind needs time to piddle and wander. When I work on a sermon or prepare for a seminar, what might take someone else two hours will take me five because I will focus awhile, then piddle around and come back to it. Then I'll stay tuned to the task for a while longer and take another break before I can move on. I have been doing exactly that while writing this. So for me even to think of the time it would take to complete a book was a very overwhelming task.

And yet I wanted to share my experiences and some things I learned with others. I wanted to make an impact on the lives of people I would never meet. The only problem was that the work to make that happen seemed like torture, and I was overwhelmed and completely shut down at the thought of it. When I thought of a book, I had thoughts and feelings of:

"It's impossible for me to sit still long enough to crank out
   a book."
"There's no way I could complete a book once I started
   it."
"I just don't think I am wired to write books. Maybe articles
   but not whole books."

None of those thoughts were about not being able to research the subject and have enough material. None of them
related to not having any good ideas worth turning into a book.
They were all about the task, the work, the process.

People out of work may feel the same way. They may not
have any doubts about whether or not they could *do* a good
job. The problem may be in just feeling overwhelmed about
the process of *getting* a good job. If you are overwhelmed
with the job of getting a job, you may have to reframe job-
getting the same way I had to reframe book-writing. Here is
what I did.

I had to admit that I could not write a book in a day, a
week, or most likely in a month. And I sure could not do it in
the one hour I had in front of me. So I had to use the principle of one to help me progress from a guy with a few ideas
about books to a guy who actually authored a book. I gave up
on writing a whole book and settled in with a goal of having
written one page of, not a book, but an outline within one
hour. I knew that I had it in me to write a one-page outline
within one hour.

So I sat down and wrote up the outline that one day would
become my first book, *Hooked on Life*. It was one of the first
books integrating recovery and addiction treatment concepts
into a Christian book. It happened once I surrendered my

need to write an entire book and focused on accomplishing one page of an outline within one hour. I added page after page until I had about a thirty-page outline.

Once I had that outline, I had a road map of a book that was very easy to follow. But I still could not sit still long enough to get the book written. It was almost as overwhelming a task as it was without the outline. The outline was more of a spotty, disjointed assignment I could easily jump around in. But writing would be much more intensive and call upon everything I had to finish.

Fortunately I had this power-of-one concept within me, and I put it to use. I could not write one full book, but I could write one full page. All I had to do to write a book was to write one page. It did not have to be perfect or even very good—it just had to be a full page. I reframed what I was doing into a process that included editors and proofreaders who would take care of the crumminess of a single page that would never happen unless I wrote it.

So one single day after another single day, I wrote one single page at a time. Some days I could actually write more than one page. By the end there were days when I accumulated ten pages. Those were amazing days all made possible because of the power of one—the power of writing one page at a time.

Discovering the Power of 1 Percent

I had the power-of-one concept within me because of another time in my life when I was stuck. At that time, I wanted to give God a portion of my money. My father drummed into me that God is the One who gave me all the money I have had, have, and will ever receive. And the least I could do was to give God back 10 percent of that money. Ten percent acknowledged that I believed in God, I knew he was the provider of all I had, and I am grateful to him. But I was just too in debt to give 10 percent.

So each month I would get a paycheck, write out my 10 percent check, and stick it into the back of the checkbook. When the checks piled up too much, I would tear them up and start over, doing the same thing. I was not managing my money well enough to give that 10 percent chunk. It could have gone on that way forever, but I finally made a life-changing decision.

I could not give 10 percent, but I could give 1 percent. I knew how to calculate one dollar out of every one hundred, and I could live without it. So I did it. And it felt so good. I went from being frustrated over what I could not do to doing what I could. I reframed the concept of giving from something my father told me to do to something I could do in my own way. The 1 percent I gave became millions of times more powerful than writing and tearing up checks for 10 percent.

I asked God to honor the 1 percent, and I was willing to make some changes so I could double 1 percent to 2 percent—and then add another powerful 1 percent on top of all that—and then double and triple and continue to give more and more of those 1 percents. Soon I was over 10 percent and loving it. It became a way of life and a way of managing my money. One percent changed everything, and the power of one can do the same thing for anyone, especially the person who is without a job.

No Way Today

If you asked me to go out and get a job when I was in my stuck stage of doing nothing and not caring, I would have felt so overwhelmed by the impossibility of the task I would probably just have done nothing. I might have gotten up and gotten busy to prove I wasn't lazy, but I would never have gotten around to doing what needed to be done to get a job. If you had met me then and tried to shame or motivate me with your words, it would not have helped. Any pressure would have been too much and I would have shut down. But there would have been something you could have done to help me, and it is what I would try to do for anyone in the same situation.

After you saturated your mind with number one, I would help you delineate the one thing you could do that would move you from doing nothing to making progress. I would give you a list of single actions to take and suggest you pick one a day for five days. Someone around you might be frustrated that in an entire workweek you did only five little things, but I would say at least you did those five things. In doing them you will have reversed a trend. You will have made a 180-degree turn by doing one thing you could. So here is a list of ten things from which I ask you to choose. Every one of them requires an action other than looking at or reading something.

Ten Healthy Choices for an Unemployed Person

1. Think of one person you know who owns or runs a business, ministry, or nonprofit organization. Call that person and either ask if he or she has any positions available or leave that question as a message.

2. Call the friend who works in the largest organization of all your friends and ask if he or she would help you get a job by introducing you to someone there.

3. Use a computer and printer to create a résumé that can be e-mailed and printed.

4. Post your résumé online in one of the job Web sites under the categories that fit you best.

5. Go online to look at some posted jobs and send your résumé to as many of them as you can in one day.

6. Buy a newspaper from your area, look at the help wanted section, and find a job you *could* do—not necessarily one that you *want* to do. See if you can set up an appointment to interview for that job.

7. Drive or take the bus to the nearest unemployment agency and take whatever time necessary to go through the interview process.

8. Identify a company you want to work for, get in the car, go there, and fill out an employment application. Ask for an interview and if there are any volunteer, apprentice, or intern positions available.

9. Call your local newspaper or go online and find out what steps you need to take to deliver papers, then take that job if it is available.

10. Follow up on one of the previous steps you have taken.

Anyone not moving forward can be helped with the simple power of one. Reframing your situation from one that is impossible to one with very possible *components* can move you to conquer things you viewed as beyond your abilities.

More Power of One

You might not be in a situation where you are stuck and cannot accomplish what you want to accomplish. The power of one could still be the number you need to reframe to get what you want in other areas of your life. Think of all the things available if we just focus on one thing versus all the overwhelming areas in our lives. One phone call can make the difference for a job. One phone call can also make the difference in reconciling with a friend. One phone call to a person you have not talked with in years could also reopen a relationship. One "I'm sorry" to a spouse could change the entire direction of the relationship.

Cleaning up one closet, organizing one desk, sweeping one garage can begin a long-overdue cleanup. Sending one letter, volunteering one hour, making one visit, or giving someone one ride can start the habit of helping others who cannot do much for themselves. One counseling appointment, one page of one book, one online search in an area you are struggling with could unlock some new ways to handle situations.

One Bible verse memorized or one page of the Bible read or one minute in prayer could be the beginning of a renewed spirituality. The hours of quiet time you can never get around to having can be replaced with a quality minute with God, either reading his Word or sharing your heart. One quality, authentic minute is far better than any number of minutes acted on under obligation or pressure. And all of this begins with this powerful number of one. Reframe that little digit to the most powerful number in the world.

Reframing Emptiness

Reframing can help a person who feels more emptiness in life than fulfillment. I used to joke about my seeing the glass as half-full rather than half-empty, but I also saw my teeth floating in the glass. As I get closer to the teeth-floating-in-the-glass stage of life, the joke becomes less and less amusing to me.

But the analogy of the glass with 50 percent of its contents and how we view it is a good one. It seems that there are those who look on the bright side of everything and those who are always playing out the worst-case scenarios in their minds. The way they observe the things in their lives and the way they explain those things to themselves, the running dialogue created inside their heads, forms a life framed in the negative, resulting in emptiness and despair.

I have often seen people in this empty state full of questions about the meaning of life, wondering whether there is even value in continuing. Sometimes they engage in destructive behaviors just to sense some life from somewhere. They might cut themselves just to feel something other than nothingness.

If this is the way you are living, it is not so much a matter of seeing your life differently but of reconstructing the frame upon which it is built. That frame is built on what you tell yourself. You might drink or drug to cope with the desperation, but you might also do it for another reason. You could be doing a number of things just to create drama.

Deadly Drama

I love to see lives changed through reframing, because up until they are, people tend to do whatever they can either to prove they are alive or in hope of someone acknowledging their existence in the midst of their struggle. I see repeated catastrophes: accident-prone bodies recovering from injury upon injury, near-death experiences from accidental overdoses and weak suicide attempts, good jobs sacrificed in a childish tirade of anger, breakups and splitups and makeups. I look at these lives and wonder, "Why all of this drama?" The drama actually becomes the point of these people's whole lives. In the drama they find a spark of life, even if the drama is a deadly run-in with an eighteen-wheeler. The drama becomes the only thing signifying they are alive and engaged at some level.

One of the saddest parts of all the drama is the aspect of wasted energy and effort. All of the struggler's resources are spent on either creating the drama or cleaning up after it. Court appearances, medical bills, insurance claims, and structural damage all require hours of attention, which, if directed elsewhere, could produce a new life of hope and meaning. Cleaning up after the curtain has dropped on another dramatic episode could be replaced with stepping up and getting out of the rut where time is wasted and life is profoundly empty.

The Internal Reframing of Emptiness

The empty life can be changed by reframing the elements comprising it. Thoughts and beliefs continuing to rattle around in the head can deepen the emptiness and produce more self-destructive behavior. We all need to examine what we are telling ourselves from time to time, but it is especially important for the person who feels life is valueless and moves from one crisis to the next. I was reminded of how important the words in our head are when my wife began hemorrhaging after the birth of our son.

Everything went well until about six hours after he was born. She got up to use the restroom and passed out as blood covered the bathroom floor. Eight nurses rushed in and quickly called for a doctor because it was obvious she was bleeding to death. I had never seen anything like this. There was more blood in one place from one person than I ever thought possible. I witnessed all of this and was not asked to leave because I was helping rather than creating another crisis.

Fortunately, I had been to a writers' workshop and met a woman who wrote a book on verbal first aid. It sounds unusual, but the premise she researched indicated that what is said to the victim of an accident or the person in the middle of a health crisis has a great deal to do with the victim's survival and recovery. She documented cases of people who were in automobile accidents who were bleeding to death. These people slowed down their bleeding when they were reassured. They were told to tell themselves everything would be okay, to get in touch with their breathing and calm down. There were many other instances demonstrating that what people around the victim said made a great difference in the outcome.

I could not do anything for my wife physically, but I could work with her mentally. I told her the doctor was confident she would be all right. I told her the nurses had things under control and she was safe. I told her to relax and not worry. Over and over I allowed her to hear my voice in a confident and caring way.

Later she told me how my voice settled her down, caused her to have hope, and removed her panic. She began to move out of her original thoughts of "I gave him a boy and now God is taking me" to thoughts of recovery and healing. She moved from apprehension to appreciation for being in a hospital when it all happened. The thoughts in her head made a difference.

Can you go from a life of emptiness to a fun and meaningful life by changing only what you say to yourself? No. But you can begin a process of moving out of a pattern of repeated drama and crisis. You can start to see and hear the world differently because the internal frame of reference is different. Reframing can replace the emptiness with a structure that leads to healthy living and looking for the good rather than waiting for the next bad thing to happen.

Unresponsive Ailments

Reframing is not a cure-all—it is not the cure for anything. It is the *beginning* of healing, and it can become a way of life just as the negative framing patterns have become a way of life for those who are stuck.

For example, anorexia should always be treated as seriously as cancer or any other life-threatening medical crisis. If it is not, the mind of the teenager can become the mind of the adult. Working with women who are continuing to struggle with anorexia and bulimia is quite frustrating. If you are one of them, you know how locked you are into your way of doing things, your way of seeing things, and your way of getting through to the next day. Adult anorexics reframe themselves every day, but the frame is always distorted. A wide jawbone becomes a sign of being too fat. A deposit of flesh becomes an excuse to

exercise for hours in an effort to cleanse the body of fat and re-
fine the apprearance. If the woman has held on to the anorexic
way of life, her body, mind, and the rest of her existence would
benefit from reframing.

Too often the work begins midstream. The focus is on feelings and behaviors, consequences and results. There is value in
backing up and taking a deeper look at what the anorexic sees,
not just in the mirror, but in other people. Hyperself-criticism
reflects a view of a world with hypercritical people who always
want better, best, and perfection. The reframing must start
with the view of the world at large before the internal world
of the anorexic can change. Reframing takes away the false beliefs, such as "All people are bad," "I will never be good or perfect enough," or "What is on the outside of my soul determines
the destiny of my life." False beliefs framing chronic struggles
must be taken apart and reconstructed in the form of a new,
healthy, and realistic frame.

Whether it is anorexia or bulimia or some other nagging
long-term problem, reframing can be the beginning of the
end of the struggle. Someone living with free-floating anxiety can be helped by reframing reality and the unrealistic
fears. Chronic depression showing no improvement even
after years of a pharmacological treasure hunt could change
with reframing. It can come down to the issue of what you
don't see rather than what you don't feel. A fellow speaker
friend of mine discovered this as he dealt with his chronic
depression. He was one of those deep-thinking, highly sensitive people who have a predisposition to depression. On
top of that, he was raised in a home with a very distant and
goal-oriented father. The father produced a process-focused
boy who was being raised by a results-minded dad. It was

not a combination that would overcome a predisposition to anything.

A Different Look at Depression

My friend went to one of the best psychiatrists in the country. I know that because I go to the same one. If anyone could lead him to the proper medication, it would have been this particular doctor. I credit this psychiatrist for keeping my friend alive during the darkest hours of his despair.

Through medication he tried to exist at a different level and through therapy he tried to work through feelings. He did a lot of grief work over the wounds from his father and the distance that would always be there. He was led to set realistic goals and to give up carrying the burdens of the world on his back. But it was in reframing his life that he finally found a way of living with his depression rather than fighting against it. When he began living with it, it no longer controlled him.

For most of his adult life, he saw himself as this sad figure who did not have what it took to live a normal life and function as other men do. He felt inferior and essentially moaned and groaned about the pitiful state of his relationship with his father. The rejection and judgment he felt from his father created deep shame within him. When his mood lifted temporarily, he really could not enjoy it because he felt it inevitably would deteriorate, and it always did. There was just not a lot right about his life, and he fought every day to stay engaged and active.

And all the while he did this, people loved to hear him speak. They connected with him deeply and felt as if he were talking to them individually, knowing their struggles and providing hope. He knew he was a good speaker, but he mostly thought that was a result of the tremendous amount of research he did before he gave a talk. All of this resulted in a very talented man who struggled for years and fought his chronic depression with everything he had.

But gradually his life began to change. He did not find a new medication; he continued on the same one he had been taking for a few years. He did not go to any breakthrough seminar or workshop that turned all the lights on for him. The work he did was mostly with a pen and a journal. He began to write the things he believed about himself and his life. He developed a list of overriding truths he incorporated into his thinking, feeling, and relating with others. He worked on his list and finally pared it down to the most significant one that exerted the most influence on his everyday life.

He shared the list with me, and here are the beliefs that had come to control him. They were the frame in which he viewed all of life:

I am not like other men.
I am inadequate.
I cannot endure the normal pressures of life.
Life is harder for me because of the way I feel about things.
My father does not care for me.
My father did not equip me for what was ahead.
My mother did not care enough to intervene with Father.
I have failed at most relationships.
Life is far more painful than I ever imagined.
If I stop fighting the sadness, it will engulf me.
People expect way too much from me.

I am living at my limit and cannot take much more.

God must be very disappointed in the way my life has turned out.

This is no way to be if I am to raise a healthy son.

I have many fears I don't fully understand.

Anyone would be angry if they had gone through some of the things I have had to experience.

That list is pretty sad. There is no upside to all of those thoughts running his life. He came to see what he was living with every day. This was the dialogue or the background music of his mind that no medication turned down or off. Facing these feelings and assumptions after writing them down helped him to clarify just how much of his life was in jeopardy because of these horrifically negative statements.

Opposite Day

Insight comes from the strangest places, and his came from his five-year-old boy. His five-year-old came home from a friend's house playing a little game most kids play. He was saying the exact opposite of what he thought and declaring it was "opposites day." So he bravely said to his father, "I don't like you, Daddy." Then a half second later, he blurted out, "Opposites day!" That went on for the rest of the day. Everything was the opposite. If something was black, he would declare it white. Some of his statements were quite amusing, including when he said, "I won't have to go to the bathroom ever again" and then ran off to go potty.

A few days later, my friend was thinking about his boy and the game gave him an idea. He took out his journal and read through each of the beliefs he was living with and thought about the opposite of each one. Then he wrote out a new list, writing the opposite of what he believed, putting a positive spin on it, or noting something good about it. Here is how his list changed:

I am not like other men.

I am a lot like other men in many ways, but what is unique about me is what I like best about myself, even if it sets me apart from other men.

I am inadequate.

To have come this far and done what I have done and survived what I have been through shows that I am a capable human being who has met many challenges most men will never have to face.

I cannot endure the normal pressures of life.

I feel things very deeply and I have proven that I can bear the burdens of others. They appreciate the fact that I connect with them at the heart of their pain.

Life is harder for me because of the way I feel about things.

I have experienced all of the dimensions of life, the depths of despair and the heights of glory, because I am willing to experience and feel all that life has to offer.

My father does not care for me.

My father is very different from me and does not really know me as a person. Although it has not been in the ways I wanted and needed, he has tried to show me that he cares greatly for me even though he does not know how to connect with me.

My father did not equip me for what was ahead.

Because my father was so caught up in his own problems, he did not take enough time to ensure I would be safe and adequate. So I learned to survive and developed strengths that I would never have had if he had raised me differently.

My mother did not care enough to intervene with Father.

My mother loved me deeply, but she did not know how to help me connect to my father or my father to connect to me. Even if she had known, she was raised in a cultural subset where women did not confront their husbands about such things.

I have failed at most relationships.

Every relationship that has been difficult has taught me something new. I have always been willing to learn, and I am better today in relationships with others than I have ever been.

Life is far more painful than I ever imagined.

I was protected from many things when I was growing up, so the reality of life was a shock to me. But I did not crawl back in a hole in the face of it. I learned to adapt to it and cope with it, even at the most painful times.

If I stop fighting the sadness, it will engulf me.

Instead of fighting the sadness, I can live with it and experience it without the fear of it taking over. It does not lead me to a place beyond my control, but it always teaches me more about myself and the people I care about. I don't have to allow it to control me or be the overriding emotion of my life.

People expect way too much from me.

People connect with me, and they appreciate my ability to understand them and help them. I don't have to respond every time someone needs someone. I am not being selfish if I take time for my own survival. People don't expect too much—I just give them more than is healthy, and I won't do that today.

I am living at my limit and cannot take much more.

I can handle many things, but there are only so many things I have to handle. I will refuse to be controlled by things, and I will deal only with the priorities of my life and family first. Then I will welcome the challenges beyond that.

God must be very disappointed in the way my life has turned out.

God knew me before he made me, and he has been there through everything. He has never let me down and has always provided for me. There is nothing I have ever done to make him love me less, and he has provided some surprises and little miracles along the way to be sure I knew he was on my side.

This is no way to be if I am to raise a healthy son.

The way I am raising my boy is not perfect, but it is adequate. He needs to be raised by a man who can teach him that life does not always go as planned. He will be aware and sensitive. He will be capable and adequate to handle the demands of manhood. He will know the reality of pain, and he will know how to handle it. He will know how to connect with the hearts of those around him. He will become a great man under my parenting and with the help of God.

I have many fears I don't fully understand.

My fears are merely reminders that I am not all-powerful—that I am not God and that I need God to help me every day. That I have moved ahead in spite of them is evidence that I am living a courageous life.

Anyone would be angry if they had gone through some of the things I have had to experience.

Anger is not very helpful to me. It cuts me off and saps my energy. I will try to understand those who trigger my anger. I will move toward forgiveness rather than revenge. I will take the role of the stronger man and refuse to be sucked into bitter dispute.

Every day my friend would review his lists. At first he would read the old thought that had been keeping him in despair. Then he would read the opposite or revision of it. He would journal about each one. Sometimes he would write a note after each one. Other times he would make a note or two of some thought on only one of the beliefs. The next day he would move on to another revised belief.

After a while, he began to read only the revised statements to himself and journal his thoughts and feelings about it. Then, in his final adjustment, he edited himself and allowed himself only to write positive and affirming things rather than focus on the negative. Little by little, he started to feel differently. And it transferred into other areas of life.

He became habitual about reframing thoughts and feelings in a more positive light. He would hear people complain about certain things, and when appropriate he would interrupt to point them toward the upside of the downside they were talking about. People began to notice. It came across as optimism and a positive attitude. He began to spend more days without depression than with it. He began to feel better about the good stuff and less bad about the negative. His life felt deeper and richer and much more authentic. But it was also more hopeful and full of many good things.

My friend continued with medication, individual therapy, and a support group. Those elements of his recovery were vital. But he experienced them all on a self-taught method of reframing everything. My friend found a way out of repeated depression and despair through reframing. If you have experienced depression that was unresponsive to medication and counseling, you might want to back up and work on the frame with which you are dealing. Perhaps retraining your brain to reframe the thoughts and feelings that are frequent invaders of your mind could be the first step toward recovery from chronic and unresponsive depression. Reframing won't cure, but it might help.

Inevitable Dilemmas

I have some friends who are adrenaline junkies. It is no less a drug to them than methamphetamines would be to someone else. They need it to survive. And they do things to "score it" on a regular basis. There are twenty-four-hour mountain-biking races, heli-skiing so dangerous one guy had to be air-lifted out because he was too afraid to go down, hang gliding, giant-wave surfing, and parachuting out of airplanes. If an activity is not a little bit on the edge, they don't really enjoy it.

I often wonder about the real reason they have for risking their lives. On the one hand, I think it must be a sort of medication against depression and anxiety, and on the other hand, I think it could be a way of proving the inevitable is not overtaking them.

All of us will experience some inevitable losses. We can jump out of airplanes to prove we are not dead yet, but we will eventually have to face the reality of some very negative events in our lives. We are getting older and with that comes some limitations. We may have the same energy to do something, but we are not as easily restored. It becomes harder to bounce back. Aging does that to everyone. You can see that as a death sentence, or you can see that as the beginning of a new phase of life.

Today I was speaking with a woman who turned sixty a couple of years ago. When it happened, she thought life as she knew it was over. She felt old and ugly and unacceptable. It was a bit of a two-thirds crisis rather than a midlife crisis. She wanted to crawl under her covers and not come out. She hit the inevitable wall of reality and had to grieve what she was and had lost while accepting what her life had become. As she focused on herself and her plight, the future did not look so very bright. But she had a change of heart and a change of vision.

The woman took in her grandson when he was a very young boy. Now he was heading to college, and he still needed her as much as he did when he was a young boy. She is his anchor, and she provides for him and encourages and challenges him to do his best. He is a great kid. So she began to reframe her life.

The frame of a glamour queen or a young hot chick that remained in her head years after she was anything close to that was replaced with a frame of being the best she could be for this boy. He became the primary relationship that motivated her to get out of bed and work. So there I was, watching her work rather than hearing she had not gotten out of bed in years. The inevitable reality of aging hit her at sixty, and rather than resign from life, she reframed her life and continues to do it every day.

Something's Gotta Give

No one is immune to the inevitable disappointments and tragedies in life. For some, it is the slow process of aging that finally can no longer be ignored. For others, a sudden tragedy becomes their biggest challenge: a stroke, heart attack, loss of a limb, or the loss of a loved one. After years of faithfulness, there may be a betrayal or abandonment. Some experience abuse and others face the tragedy of losing everything of material value. Mistakes of others and mistakes of our own pile on top of each other and force us to live in the residue of impulsive, addictive, and damaging choices. This is what we all face while we chase our dreams and wish upon stars that too often fall right back in our laps. Sooner or later, something is going to hit and hit us hard.

When tough things happen to us, we can weep, moan, and wail about the unfairness of life and about our strange ability to be victimized by it over and over again. We can succumb to it if we believe each tragedy is part of our identity or makes a statement about us. In other words, if we personalize each sad event or development, it can become a much more powerful force to our detriment than it has to. Reframing can prevent that from happening.

Framing and Reframing Life's Tough Developments

Here is how we might frame the disappointments that pile up on us:

God must be punishing me.

I must be a pretty bad person to have brought this on myself.

Nothing good happens for me.

The rest of my life is going to be one disappointment after another.

I just don't have what it takes as other people my age do.

I am feeling more worthless than ever.

I might as well give up.

Filling the mind with these kinds of thoughts can send us further down the path of despair and hopelessness. They leave us empty and feeling inadequate, singled out, and deserving of only negative consequences. The negativity feeds upon itself, and we actually produce more disasters coupled with extremely negative feelings about life and ourselves. If we don't reframe the disappointments and disasters, they will define our lives and destroy the possibilities for more meaning and purpose in our lives.

Here is how these disappointments can be reframed:

God must be punishing me.

God is love and he loves me. Ever since Adam had a fruit snack, we have all had to deal with the downside of life. It isn't personal, it is just the reality of a fallen world. If I trust God and rely on him and some helpful friends, I will grow from this and God will use it. God is not through with me yet.

I must be a pretty bad person to have brought this on myself.

I have some crummy stuff in me as everyone has. And just like everyone else, I make mistakes. If I brought this on myself, then I can change whatever it was that led to this. If I had nothing to do with this, I can at least learn from it and share my soul with others who will have to go through this also.

Nothing good happens for me.

A lot of good things have happened to me, and I have caused many good things to happen. From time to time I may go through a season where it is difficult to focus on the good things. It is just a season. It will pass. I can endure it and become a better person as a result.

The rest of my life is going to be one disappointment after another.

> *As I get older, there are going to be more and more physical limitations on my body. I will lose close friends and life will change. But I can move out of my self-obsession and see how much of myself I can give away during the time I have left. I can reach out to others and help them deal with their difficulties. My body may have more and more limitations, but the opportunities of my heart are limitless. I can do more worthwhile and meaningful things that will never disappoint me.*

I just don't have what it takes as other people my age do.

> *Things may not have been as easy for me as they have been for others, but I have made it through it all and come out on the other side. Some of those who are on top would not have handled what I have had to deal with as well as I have. I have had courage, and no matter what my limitations, I have always done the best I could with what I had. If I am limited in some way, I will seek out the friends and supporters that can help me grow in any area of weakness.*

I am feeling more worthless than ever.

> *Feelings are part of my life, but they are not the ultimate focus of my life. I may feel worthless due to a recent setback, but I have value as a child of God. When I feel worthless, I can still do worthwhile things. I can still reach out to others with compassion, listening to what they are struggling with and helping them move beyond their hurts.*

I might as well give up.

I have felt like giving up before, but each time I have refused. I refuse to do so now. When I persevere, something amazing always happens that reminds me I need to move on and get beyond whatever is overwhelming me. I will not give up. Instead I will give myself away to others who might feel like giving up also. Tomorrow will be a better day, and I will be here to experience it.

Reframing is an ongoing process that can benefit all of us. It can lead us out of our troubles and into the lives of others who need help. It is a way to step back and take a second look at our present circumstances. Once we see what is before us, we can talk to ourselves in positive and encouraging ways. We can also begin to see things from the perspective of others and even God. We can treat ourselves with respect by reframing the inside with respectful thoughts and positive feelings. And if we do it long enough, it will become second nature to us when we encounter the downside of life.

CHAPTER FOUR

What Reframing Determines

My Friend Brad

Reframing your life is a different way of looking at your past, a unique way of dealing with the present, and a healthy way of facing the challenges of the future. When you start reframing certain events or areas of your life, it is not long before you are living a lifestyle where reframing becomes a way of life. I liken that lifestyle, in many ways, to how my friend Brad does his job as a Newport Beach policeman.

Brad is one of the greatest men walking the face of the planet. He is a phenomenal Christian man who lives the Christian life as few I have known. A loving husband and father who has made great decisions, he has led his family out of a very tiny condo into a spacious and beautiful home—all on a policeman's salary. If you knew my friend Brad, I am sure you would respect him as much as I do. Years ago I bought him the pistol he carries. He named it Steve. So, you criminals look out for Steve and Brad.

I believe one of the reasons Brad does so well in his private life is because the way he functions on the job has seeped into his home life. He has a mind-set that leads to good decisions because he is able to see the whole picture. On patrol, if Brad wants to have an easy shift, all he has to do is stay in one place, not look around, not notice what people are doing, drink coffee, then punch out at the end of the shift. If he worked that way, he would never get involved with a conflict or have to go to the trouble of filling out a lot of paperwork because he arrested someone or gave out a ticket. If he worked that way, he would not be doing a very good job at all.

Many of us go through our lives just like that. We look the other way. We don't get involved. We don't trouble ourselves to do the difficult things we need to do. We would not make very good policemen. Some of the saddest stories I have heard have been from daughters who were abused by their fathers. Now that is sad enough, but when the stories involves mothers who knew it was happening and looked the other way, the sorrow is so deep. I have heard these mothers say they knew it was occuring, in some way there was an awareness of it, but they did nothing. One woman said it took the pressure off her as a wife to do what she did not want to do. So she sacrificed her daughter for her own relief.

Stop Looking at the Tops of Your Shoes

If you are in the midst of something you know is not right and you have decided to look the other way, thinking it is not your responsibility, it is not that bad, it will just go away, you need to reframe the way you think. You must start to think like Brad. It is your job as an adult to look around. It is your job to be aware.

It is your job to notice. That is the first step in reframing your whole life. You have to decide that the few or many areas you have neglected must no longer be overlooked. You have a job to do for yourself, your family, and your friends. You must stop looking at the top of your shoes and look up and around you.

There are things you can do to make today a better day if you notice them. There are actions you can take to secure a better future for yourself if you will become aware of things you have been choosing to let slide.

These things might be financial, they might be health related, they might involve your kids or spouse or the person you are dating. You have to become the policeman of your life, and that means you have to look and listen and notice all that is going on in your life.

What I am addressing is the issue of responsibility. Irresponsible people have a way of framing life to make the short-term challenges easy to deal with. They use phrases inside their heads like these:

That is not really that important.
I can do that later.
I have a lot more important things to do.
I am not in charge of that.
Even if I wanted to, I couldn't do much about it.
I have let it go this far, so there isn't much I can do now.
I am just too overwhelmed to deal with that.

This kind of thinking and perspective gets you off the hook if and when you do notice that something is not exactly right. This mind-set must be reframed and every one of these assumptions must be changed and reframed from a "do nothing" slant to a "do something" attitude. It is your life, and it is a gift. You are in charge, and you must stop turning it over to others or to "fate" and become engaged in all that is going on.

You must look around at your life, and you must take action when it is needed. Otherwise you are going through life waiting for the next shoe to drop. You are biding your time until the next bad blow comes along and hurts you again. If this is how you are living, you would not make a very good policeman, and you are not making a very good future for yourself.

The Reframed Mind

The practice of reframing eventually rewires your mind. You don't just see things differently, you are wired differently as you encounter new challenges. You end up with a better brain. One of the things Brad has to give up as a police officer is taking everyone and everything at face value. He is a very positive person with a great outlook on life when he is at home. But on the job he has to assume someone is motivated to get him off track and to overlook a big chunk of reality.

When he stops people and asks if they have been drinking, it would sure be nice and easy to always believe what they say. It would be effortless just to say, "Okay, have a nice day. Sorry to bother you," after people who swerved into oncoming traffic said they had only one glass of wine with dinner. But that is not going to save lives and get drunk persons off the road. So Brad hears what the people are saying but assumes it might not be the whole picture. The drivers might have had only had a couple of glasses of wine. But there is a good chance, based on the swerve, that the two glasses of wine were on top of a six-pack of beer or a slew of mixed drinks. So Brad goes to the trouble to see if there is substance behind what the drivers said. Perhaps they are not drunk, and the steering wheel just slipped when they were distracted. So he observes the speech pattern, listens for slurs and inconsistencies, and eventually asks the people to prove they are sober enough to drive. His awareness leads to action, and the action leads to a safer world. It is the way the man's mind is structured and framed.

We all need to be more like Brad. We need to be aware of what is going on around us. The reframed mind is able to see because it wants to see and it thrives on being aware. The reframed mind sees reality and intervenes in it where appropriate. Responsible action for self, family, and friends replaces irresponsible procrastination and good intentions. Concentration is possible. Focus is sharpened, and the substance of thoughts and feelings changes. Out of this different mindset a whole new way of living emerges. Not quickly and not easily—but eventually people wake up and realize they have taken charge of their lives. They see the world differently, and they act on it in responsible ways.

Reframed Relationships

A reframed mind can more easily develop and maintain healthy relationships. When relationships are broken, reframing can help mend them. It can do that most effectively when the reframing moves beyond the big "I" and focuses on the plight of others. When people give up their anger just long enough to peer into the hearts of others, it can make all the difference in the world and restore relationships that could have remained broken forever. This is not easy—humility and a surrendered heart are required to make it work—but when it does, the best surprises can result.

I was speaking at a large conference one day on getting into the shoes of the person who offended you. I was challenging people hurt in the worst of ways to do the unimaginable and try to take the side of the person who hurt them, just to see if it would help them move beyond the event.

As I was speaking, I thought of how this must be sounding to someone abused as a child by a parent or a woman whose husband ran off with someone much younger. But I knew that even in those cases, sometimes this exercise can unlock a person's continuing to focus on the other and then move on. The exercise is not intended to justify or rationalize what was done in any way. It is intended to humanize the offender so forgiveness can be more easily rendered. Simply put, you can't forgive a devil, but you can forgive a person consumed by a sickness.

Jewelry and Jail

After I presented this most delicate concept, trying not to negate the very accurate feelings of blame placed on the perpetrator, I was prepared for some people to be a bit rattled and challenge my approach. But that didn't happen. Instead a couple approached and asked if they could have a word with me. I actually had all the time in the world that day, and I told them so. They poured out their hearts about the tragedy that occurred in their family. It all revolved around a mail-order jewelry business they started back in the seventies, which did quite well thanks to the creativity of the woman and the tight-fisted management of the man. That little business provided them with more than their dreams. They had the freedom to be their own bosses and travel and live as very few are able to do.

Their son did not want to be in the jewelry business and became a lawyer, eventually starting his own firm and working as his own boss also. Their daughter was interested in the business and began working with them right out of college. As the parents progressed in years, they gave her more responsibility in hopes that one day she would take over and they could retire with a lot of years left to enjoy life together. All seemed to be going pretty well until an annual audit revealed something very disturbing. Over a period of the previous two years, three hundred thousand dollars had been taken out of the company.

To the father, this was incomprehensible. He knew where every penny was spent—at least he thought he did. Hearing the news, he immediately called in his daughter to ask her why she had not told him, and she explained that she was hoping to figure out where the money went and perhaps even get it back before he had to be troubled by it all. She said she felt she was making progress in following the path left by the culprit who embezzled the money.

The father did not care what she *thought*—this was about a lot of money. He called in a group of auditors to investigate every transaction until they knew for sure where the money had gone. When the dust settled, the missing money, and perhaps more than they had originally uncovered, had gone into an account managed by the daughter. The couple's own flesh and blood embezzled the money from them.

The parents did what they would have done had it been anyone else. They called the district attorney, turned over the evidence, and pressed charges against her. She pleaded no contest and served six months in jail. When she was released, she was no longer part of the family. The mother and father disowned her and told her they did not want to see her again.

The separation was to be final and complete, but there was a problem that became worse and worse as the separation grew longer. Neither the mother or father could sleep. What was once easy for them became a nightly ritual of tossing, turning, pacing, and just trying to get through another miserable night. Their nights and their days were consumed with the anger they had toward their daughter and the complete lack of gratitude and loyalty she displayed. Their hurt was very deep, and it just continued to get worse. By the time they heard my talk on reframing, they were more miserable than they had ever been in their lives.

Two Reframed Hearts

Rather than complain to me that it would be impossible to do anything but see their daughter for what she was, an ungrateful criminal, they told me they were both very moved by my talk. They realized they were carrying a justifiable resentment. They saw that they held onto their anger because they felt they were entitled to it, and they arrogantly pushed their daughter out of the family. Stubborn resistance to her attempts at reconciliation landed them on their feet at night, unable to rest body, mind, or soul. They looked back and forth at each other during the talk, acknowledging areas in which they were stuck. When I asked them to step into her shoes, they did. The father explained he saw her in a totally different light.

Before the talk he saw her as a vicious, ungrateful, and unloving woman who didn't care about them or anyone in the family. He saw her as someone who set out to hurt the very people who brought her into the world and provided for her. In his mind, she was all bad because you would have to be all bad to betray your own parents and steal from them. But through the talk the father started writing some notes as his wife watched.

When he was done, they had both reframed their girl from their own reframed hearts. They came to see her as something other than a criminal who set out to hurt them. Instead he took some responsibility for her desperation. He paid her about a third of what others in her position made, thinking that would make her tougher and she would appreciate more of what she had when she took over. So he figured she was taking what she thought she was owed, what would one day be hers. It was probably a gradual thing, starting with small amounts that just kept getting bigger and bigger. When she had confessed to what she did, she told him it was about much more than the money. She had come to discover she felt robbed by both of them when she was younger. The time they spent working, talking about work, and traveling was time when she felt neglected. She said it became a compulsive action, triggered each time they left her in charge of the operation. When she shared this, all he could say was a very loud *"Bull!"*

Now he could see what she had been trying to explain. She was not justifying the wrong thing as right, she was just trying to help them see how something so ugly could spring up inside her. She was not blaming them, she was just trying to help them believe she did not hate them, nor had she wanted to hurt them. She felt stupid and deserving of everything bad that happened to her, but at the time, all they felt was that she sounded as if she was blaming them. They could not accept that explaining is not the same as blaming or justifying or minimizing what happened.

Now, regardless of what she actually believed, they felt they had treated her too harshly and the two of them were paying a high price as a result. They had gone too far in their vindictiveness toward her, and they were ready to do something very different.

The couple decided to go home and write their daughter a letter, telling her they made a mistake. They had been too harsh and hard. They wanted her back as their daughter. All was forgiven, and they were ready to start over if she was.

It was a dramatic change of heart, and what I loved hearing was they already felt a two-ton burden lift off their hearts. They already felt relief, and even if she did not respond, they felt they had gotten out of their own shoes and into hers and responded more the way Jesus would want. I don't know what the result was when they contacted their daughter, but I could see there was already a result inside them.

This example of reframing a relationship is very dramatic and extreme. So was one of the most famous stories Jesus ever told—the parable of the prodigal son. If I were writing the story of the prodigal son today, I could give it one of several different titles: "The Ungrateful Brother" would work if I focused on this brother who would one day have to split everything the father had all over again. "The Celebration" would work if I focused on how exciting it is to see someone who was lost to the world return. But I would want to title it *The Reframed Father*, and I would focus on how that man reframed all the anger he was entitled to have and all the judgment he was entitled to give and ended up wanting his boy back more than anything.

So when that boy headed over the hill, Dad was waiting and running to greet him.

If reframing can help in these very dramatic instances, it can help in everyday life when the little things crop up and want to become really big issues that will hamper us. We can reframe irritating things as normal results of relationships, opportunities to give grace, experience growth, and mature. We can reframe disappointments as part of everyone's life and not believe we are unique or singled out or being punished. We can try to find the humor in it all rather than find the things in which we know we are right and focus on those.

It is our choice how we see things and the light we allow them to cast upon our lives. We can reframe the small things, move beyond them, and grow through them to experience deeper and more connected relationships, or we can allow them to keep us focused on the superficial and never move beyond the surface and the small things that don't feel good at the time. Reframing the small things that *can* hurt us will prevent them from becoming bigger things that *will* hurt us.

Reframing for a Healthy Life

It seems as if almost every day I come across a new study in *USA Today*, the *New York Times*, *O, The Oprah Magazine*, or *Reader's Digest* that confirms the state of our minds and hearts has a lot to do with how healthy we live. Angry people have heart attacks. Depressed people have low immunity. Anxious people pump glucocorticoid hormones through their bodies, which wears them out from all the stress. In all my years of reading magazines, researching various health topics, and getting some really good information from my friends via e-mail, I don't recall anything anywhere that suggested if we hold on to our grudges, live our lives full of fear, or slump around just waiting for the next shoe to drop, our health is improved greatly. None of these things is good for us. All of them are bad for us to be living through. We can choose to live in a different way, but it will take some reframing.

Here are some thoughts and feelings that might be determining the frame in which your health hangs and some different concepts that might help in reframing your health:

I have a crummy set of genes, and I am going to be sick just like my parents were.

No matter what genes were handed down to me, I can make a difference in my health with my attitude. I can eat better than my parents knew how to eat or taught me to eat. I can exercise wisely in ways they would never have attempted. I can find new ways to cope with stress other than worrying, drinking, eating, stewing, or any of the things I watched them do.

I have always been a bit down at every stage of my life.

The reason I have been down is that I have always looked on the dark side. I have never tried to see the bright side of things. I have lived disconnected and prevented myself from experiencing many happy moments with others. I can start attending some groups where I will be cared for and loved. I can look up from the pavement and into the eyes of others and benefit from their love and care. If I need medication, I can finally be willing to take it. If I need to stop drinking to start living, I can do that also. I can change the way I view my life and the lives of others.

I can make a difference in how I feel and the level of health at which I function.

My loneliness is what keeps me locked up and in bed so much.

I am lonely because I have been waiting for people to show me they care about me even though I have not shown I care about them. I can reverse that. I can get out of this bed, and I can go and see someone. I can pay a visit to someone in worse shape than I, and I can pick up my spirits by picking up theirs. Rather than wait for someone to reach out to me, I can reach out to others.

Even if I can't get out of bed, I can pick up the phone and call. And if that fails, I can pick up a pen and write a letter that might change someone else's whole day or week. I do not have to be like this. And if I am unable to carry out what I intend to do, I can ask for support from someone else who can help me do what I cannot do on my own.

Think-Feel-Act-Feel-Think

How we think about ourselves has a lot to do with how we feel both emotionally and physically. Feeling all the negatives wears us down and out and deteriorates our health slowly but surely. It causes us to retreat and isolate and become inactive. Inertia leads to darker feelings and obsessions of the mind. Worry and physical complaints come to dominate our minds and sicken our bodies.

Doctors tell us something has to change. They put us on diets we hate and can't follow, or they tell us to exercise in ways we have no intention of following. They expect us to do what they say because they are doctors, but if we are stuck emotionally, we don't have the ability to just up and change so dramatically, even if we want to.

Whatever It Takes

Reframing can redirect so much of our lives if we can turn off the resistance to a point where we are willing to do whatever it takes to make a change. What we tend to do is frame our situations in an "all I have to do" perspective, thinking there is only one thing that must be changed, and once we accomplish that, everything else will fall in place. Many overeaters stay fat because of "all I have to do" thinking: "All I have to do is eat a salad at lunch." "All I have to do is skip breakfast." "All I have to do is eat slower." These are simplistic lies to a very complex dilemma. When we are willing to do whatever it takes, real change occurs.

In working with people who want to lose weight, I often see people turn to surgery, thinking all they have to do is have an operation and the weight falls off and stays off. But that's a sure sign that if the person does have the surgery, it will be only a matter of time before he or she is heavy again. When people resort to surgery, they can succeed if they are willing to do whatever it takes to become new people. In the beginning, the results come 100 percent from the surgery. But as strength builds, lifestyle changes must be implemented because pretty soon it is going to be a fifty-fifty proposition between the surgery and your own efforts at weight control. Then it will once again become 100 percent what you do and eat that determines your weight and ongoing success.

There is no quick fix, and it is especially not surgery. I don't think morbidly obese people should be allowed to have surgery unless they are willing to do the following:

- Agree to a balanced diet low in complex carbohydrates.
- Agree to begin an exercise program that starts slowly and gently, incorporates weight training, aerobics, and a commitment to improving all levels of fitness.
- Agree to have and be able to afford more surgery to cut away the excess skin that could hamper the patient's recovery.

When people are willing and can do all those things, there is a good chance the surgery will benefit them.

But if they are willing to do these on a regular basis, there is really little need to have the surgery. The point is, weight comes off when there is a willingness to do whatever it takes. Problems get resolved when we develop a willingness to do whatever it takes. That willingness allows us to reframe our experiences and our lives and then live the lives we have been looking for. Whether it is the weight on our bodies or feeling the weight of the world, reframing can begin the process of experiencing the light of day and enjoying every minute of it.

CHAPTER FIVE

What Reframing Is Not

Now, hopefully you have a good handle on all the forces blocking the reframing process and who can benefit from it. Before we move into how to apply the reframing process to your life, it is important to clarify what it is not, to set up a baseline of understanding that differentiates reframing from other practices. Once we do this, we will move on to the actual process of reframing your life.

The most important differentiation to make is between reframing and thinking positively. Positive thinking can help you develop an attitude that anticipates the best in people and events. If you are a habitually negative thinker, it can help you try to overlook the negatives that tend to consume all of your thinking. Being a positive versus a negative thinker would be an improvement, but it has some limitations.

Positive Thinking

If someone worked for an extremely self-obsessed and difficult boss who created a workplace fraught with at least one daily egocentric crisis, it could lead a person to dread work, resent having to earn a living, and anxiously awaiting the five o'clock whistle to blow. I have been in one of these situations, going to lunch daily with the countess of doom, and it was not fun. For a while I could not figure out why my jaw hurt all the time. That was before I discovered I had developed a nice case of TMJ from the tense eating habits I developed during hundreds of lunches with this person.

Nothing I did helped change this situation. I talked to her, tried to get her to see things from a real human being's point of view, but nothing could budge her. So I gave up on her, and as a last resort I tried to conquer the situation with a daily dose of positive attitude. For a while I felt better, overlooking the little things she did that drove everyone crazy, including noticing if I was five minutes late. I just let things go and looked at the bright side of it all.

Positive thinking is often based on a fantasy of how things could be but will never be. I created scenarios in my mind of her realizing what she did and her boss recognizing I was the one who led her to understand her problems and promoted me over her. It was a fantasy based on a false belief that this woman wanted things to change and would respond to insight that would make it happen. But she did not want things to change. She spent her life looking at all things through a controlling and self-serving eye and no amount of effort on my part was going to change her grim reality into my fantasy.

But I continued to be as positive as possible and tried to

look at all the benefits I was realizing. I saw how the difficult circumstance would help me grow in patience and show me a lot of things I should avoid if I was to win the respect of people who would work for me. No matter what she threw at me, I just smiled and thought to myself about how much more I could take and how strong I was becoming. I saw the situation as a character-building time and tried to focus on everything positive I could.

The problem was that it was such a bad situation, I did not have enough willpower to sustain the positive thinking. And it changed nothing in an ongoing situation. Eventually some people who worked for her in another department revolted, the corporate powers sided with them, and she lost her job. The woman had not earned her employees' respect, which rendered her unable to lead. Positive thinking helped some, but it did not change the situation.

Reframing might have. Had I reframed my role, I might have made a difference. Had I seen my role as something God elected me to, I would not have feared for my job. I would not have been so "nice" and would have been more up-front with her about our loss of respect for her. Had I reframed my position as one God placed me in rather than seeing it as a job I won and needed to keep, everything might have been different. I probably would have been more con-structive and less passive. I would have lived my life differ-ently rather than just trying to see it differently. I would not have beat around the bush as much. I would have been as direct with her as God is with me through his Word. Positive thinking helped me cope for a while, but reframing could have helped everyone involved.

Perhaps the biggest difference between reframing and

positive thinking is the issue of the head and the heart. Positive thinking involves the head. It is all about processing information in a new way, sometimes denying the negative truth and using the brain to conjure up positive thoughts in the midst of the negative. Add a bright smile to the mind looking for the upside of everything and you will be equipped to take on the day with a positive attitude. Reframing is much more than this kind of slanted effort. Reframing is about the heart, rather than the head. It involves how a person feels as well as thinks. It involves the character of the person, not just what thoughts he or she paints positively in his or her brain.

Ignoring Hurts and Pains

You can't reframe your life by ignoring hurts and pains that have had a significant impact on your life. Ignoring them would be a step backward toward living in denial. There would be no resolution or closure if everything unpleasant was brushed aside and negated. The feelings of hurt and pain are real, and they serve a purpose. They are healthy indicators that something unhealthy has happened and needs to be resolved. Rather than deny these emotions, reframing uses the power of those emotions to initiate change, leading to emotional strength, stamina, and personal growth.

When crummy things happen that inflict pain upon us, there is no way we can just think our way out of the pain. Many people try to do this. My father was like this. He was very big on moving on. He chose not to dwell on painful things. His strength was keeping on the path and moving forward no matter what happened. His weakness came out of that strength. There were things that needed to be processed and grieved.

He did not do a lot of that—at least if he did, I did not see it. I think this could be why he is the only one of five brothers who has died. He is the middle brother, and his untimely heart attack was more than ten years ago. He had a bright outlook, was always moving on, but there must have been some very heavy burdens his positive attitude just would not overcome. Real pain takes more than just thinking beyond the pain. Reframing leads to resolving, not just rethinking the pain all of us are forced to feel.

Negating the Past

Every person's past is a powerful force that influences current decisions and relational dynamics in everyday experiences. Reframing does not negate the reality or power of the past. It is not a means for acting as if the past never occurred. There are many approaches to problems that essentially do just that. I have seen therapists who just wanted to focus on relational and communication skills, avoiding dealing with some very important issues developed in the past.

I have always felt the way to connect deeply with people is to know what has hurt them deeply. This is something I have failed to do in past relationships and am committed to doing in the future. I don't want to relive the past or push a person back into the past, but awareness of what was there can make all the difference in the world. Blindness to the past can also make a very negative difference.

One young lady came to me struggling with her ability to connect with men. If there were ten levels in the deepest relationships, she felt she could reach only about level four. From there she guarded and protected herself, unwilling to open up to future hurts. She limited her vulnerability to hurt. Thinking positively about men and these relationships would have done nothing for her. It would have been a superficial attempt to fix a pattern that was obvious enough for her to recognize it. There had to be something in the past that would help her connect better with the men she had no trouble attracting or getting to know to a certain level.

As we discussed her life experience, it became obvious why she could have difficulty with men at the deeper levels. First of all she was adopted, so there was a vague sense that the first man in her life had not accepted her or been able to handle all of who she was. Then the parents who adopted her were in constant conflict and eventually divorced. She always felt if her adoptive father had been stronger or better, he could have prevented the divorce. He was the second male to fail her at some level. But more than that, throughout the conflict between her parents, her father was careful not to be negative about her mother, even though the mother was unfaithful and angry and very disconnected. So the father was guarded in his interaction with her. In other words, the one man she connected with could go only so deep in his own turmoil. That left her holding him responsible and never sensing a full connection between the two of them, even into her late teens.

As we processed all this, it became evident the loving relationship her father had with her helped her to be comfortable with men and have many healthy male friendships. But the real or imagined abandonments and disappointments by the first two key men in her life led to great caution with deeper relationships. The lack of an involved mother and the reality of a withholding father left her without the proper tools for connecting deeper. These were important patterns in her past. There was no way just thinking about them differently was going to help her. But reframing each new relationship with a man did help.

She began to reframe each new relationship as something other than the potential life partner she sought. Instead, she reframed each experience as a time to put something into the life of the other person while she learned to grow deeper and trust more. She kept a diary to assist her with her reframing project, plotting how deeply she felt she was sharing her feelings and how vulnerable she was when she was on a date.

This reframing lessened her anxiety while on a date. She was no longer worried about her lack of depth—she was doing something about it. She did not spend her time worrying about whether or not he liked her. She focused on and practiced being vulnerable when she was with someone who seemed safe. Essentially she stretched her "vulnerability muscles" and learned to connect on deeper levels.

While she did her exercises, she was setting an example with the guys she dated. It was more than just all about her. It became about those young men also. She became very good at sharing without appearing needy or too invasive. Once she realized she learned from the exercise, she went back to the man in her past, her father, and went to work on him. She started talking to him in different ways, sharing herself and asking him deeply probing questions. She came to understand the harshness with which he was raised and the emotional desert of his family. As their talks continued, she held no grudge and expected less and less from him while enjoying their times more than ever.

She did not ignore or negate her past; she worked with the results of her past and used the growth to contribute to her own life and the lives of those around her. Pretty soon she was living a lifestyle of intimate connection and the promotion of growth in those around her. She acknowledged the reality of her superficial experiences and then worked to create a meaningful future out of a past that left her too shallow in her connections.

Forgetting about You

In the Christian faith, a misunderstanding of certain concepts can lead to great difficulty. An easy one to understand is the misconception that I should allow God to do everything for me. Only a very ill or misguided person would come to believe that means he can lie in bed, not work, and wait for God to provide everything he needs. Turning our lives over to God does not mean to stop using our best efforts to do what we can do in this world while trusting God to help us do what we cannot.

A more difficult concept is the one of self-sacrifice. We are called to lay down our lives for another person. We are encouraged to sacrifice for someone else and not to focus on ourselves. If we take that to the unhealthy extreme, we would go into business with the person who has the most difficulty succeeding. We would marry the person who has the least chance of making it in a marriage. We would give up our right for a happy marriage so someone else could experience it at our expense. That makes no sense because God does not cause us to turn off our reasoning and decision-making abilities when we are faced with choices in life.

If we find ourselves forgetting ourselves to the detriment of our future, we need to take a second look at what we are doing. If we are making harmful decisions with regard to relating to someone who is harmful, then we are not reframing—we are forgetting to take care of ourselves so we can live long lives with purpose and meaning, serving God and others.

The other day I was talking to a man who was devastated at the loss of his girlfriend. He cared for her deeply but she did not want to go forward with the relationship. If ever a man sounded heartbroken, it was he. I felt for him because in the beginning it sounded like he lost someone who cared for him deeply. But as we talked further, he revealed something shocking. The lady he was so fond of left him to pursue a relationship with another woman.

That stopped me in mid-consoling sentence. I asked him, "Do you think it a bit strange you care deeply about someone who does not care deeply about you? Who does not care deeply about men? Who does care deeply about women? Who is out of your reach and a near, if not total, impossibility for a meaningful relationship?"

As we talked we saw he had this naïve view that if she experienced him as the man he is, she would change. It was very much like a woman who thinks she can love a man into shape once they marry. He was like a female who puts up with abhorrent behavior, believing it will all get better once they consume a piece of wedding cake. This man wanted to save this woman and felt his manhood could do it.

I told him how shocked I was. I told him I could see his being sad over a relationship not working out, especially one where all his needs were being met. But in this case he was forgetting about himself and on a mission. I encouraged him not to use marriage as a mission.

We also explored what in him was attracted to those who are impossible to have. Soon he was able to see it was all a repeat of his life with his mom. She was never available to him. Her depression made her impossible to relate to. She forgot about his needs, and now as an adult he was forgetting about them while enabling another person to forget him as a human being. That was not reframing, that was repeating the past.

Staying the Victim

Perhaps the greatest advantage to reframing your life is that it is not about staying in the role of a victim. It does not, in any way, justify past hurts or people in the present who might continue to be emotionally or physically abusive. There is nothing in reframing that would justify a person's staying put and being abused but looking at it differently.

Reframing is the opposite of inertia. It does not allow anyone to take advantage of you through a pseudo-spiritual concept or clearly harmful behavior. It sees the past in a way that can free you from it rather than relive it. It is a way of interacting in the present where there is mutuality in a relationship. It is the refusal to see yourself as anything but deserving of God's best and charting a course to live as his unique creature—victim of no one, especially of yourself and your past.

CHAPTER SIX

What Reframing Is

You Have a Clue

I have not waited until you were three-fourths of the way through the book to finally unveil what reframing is all about. While I was presenting the roadblocks and who benefits from reframing and what reframing is not, I was laying out various aspects of reframing your life. If you have connected with what I have been trying to convey, you are aware that reframing your life takes work. It is painful, and you have to give up some things you feel are entitlements, like ongoing resentment. Reframing is not something that happens overnight, and moving toward a future of becoming all God wants you to be will involve all of who you are.

Hopefully, you already understand exactly what a reframed life is all about, and you have started to reframe some things that have stuck with you and produced some unpleasant results. Whether that has happened or not, in the following pages we will look at what reframing is and what it can do for you in some very important areas of your life.

Reframing Is Living with Deep Wisdom

Have you ever walked away from a conversation and realized that what you were saying was absolutely wrong? There was some part of the story or situation that you were not aware of, and because of that you said some pretty insensitive or dumb things. You might have told someone to "just hang in there and pray and God will make it all work out," not realizing the person was living with someone who was physically abusive, and she needed to do more than endure the problem.

On our radio show I work with some of the wisest men alive today. They know God's Word, and they know how to apply biblical principles to real life problems. On our program, the Christian life intersects with some pretty tough reality, and these men and one woman have answers rich in wisdom. I often feel so inferior to their great minds when I give my perspective and then listen as they hit the major issue. It is not very enjoyable to feel unwise.

Many people go through life without the wisdom that can come from understanding their own situation today and the past from which it came. They rock along with a superficial understanding of life, never probing deeper to find the truth that leads to a more satisfying and realistic life. Wisdom does not just happen; it is acquired through time by knowing and applying truth. Just knowing without applying is worthless. Living truth produces the life that is full and rich because life is not lived on the surface. The Bible is a strong advocate for acquiring wisdom (Prov. 3:13–15):

> Happy is the person who finds wisdom and gains understanding.
> For the profit of wisdom is better than silver, and her wages are better than gold.
> Wisdom is more precious than rubies; nothing you desire can compare with her.

Clearly there is nothing more valuable than wisdom, so we should seek to build a life of wisdom. Reframing is a plan to develop wisdom from the Bible and apply it to your life. Once it forms the foundation of your decisions, you become a wise person who is able to reframe the past, current problems, and issues that arise in the future. One of my chief motivators of writing this book was to help you become a wiser person.

Full Truth

We all know what half-truth is. It is a lie containing some element of truth. Anyone who uses half-truth cannot be trusted. Full truth is not just the opposite of deceptive half-truth. Full truth is knowing a complete truth about something so it can be fully understood. It is taking a second and deeper look rather than making assumptions based on just a few facts.

If you were to buy a car and all you knew about it were a couple of truths, you might end up making a very bad purchase. It might be true that it looks really good, and it might be true the price is very low. That is not half-truth, that is truth.

But the smart buyer goes beyond knowing what it looks

like and costs. The wise person finds out the history of the car. Perhaps the price is low because that particular make has had numerous problems. Perhaps it is a used car that looks good because it was freshly painted after it was totalled and rebuilt. Full truth leads to decisions in car buying that are wise.

There may be many areas of your life where you have "bought" something because you knew the truth about it, but you did not know the full truth. There were elements you were unaware of and maybe never considered. When you bring the full truth, or as much of the full truth, out as possible, you have the opportunity to accurately frame.

Therefore, in reframing we are looking for truth so we can live more wisely and understand more fully all that has gone on, is going on, and will go on in our lives. Operating with this level of awareness leads to living with deep wisdom, a way of life that leads to a deep peace and even deeper relationships. Living without wisdom leads to superficial assumptions and judgments that disconnect us from others and reality.

The Frigid Wife

What a horrible description of a woman. When I see this phrase, I think of a person who is so prim and proper she is unwilling to leave her comfort zone and enter into a great sex life full of excitement and fulfillment. I think of someone who is afraid and uptight, who lives a very boring and protected life. I think of someone who is uninformed about sex and does not realize what a gift it is and how natural it is for humans to want to have sex and enjoy it. I think of someone who is really into herself and has not learned how to unselfishly share herself with another.

That is a pretty ugly frame to put around someone. It is a

pretty ugly label, and once you affix it to a woman, it is difficult to completely remove it and make judgments without being tainted by it. And for a woman to hear this about herself can increase her defensiveness and cause her to withdraw more, fear more, and protect herself even more. It can up the anxiety scale for a deeply anxious person who has a difficult time feeling free and letting go.

Regarding most women who could be called frigid there is a completely different frame that can change everything. It is the discovery of the full truth rather than just focusing on a symptom of the full truth. When a man focuses on the symptom, frigidity, he may be totally consumed with what he deserves and needs from her sexually. He may be expressing his frustration for her being so unresponsive to his sexual demands. If that is the case, he may miss the person he is married to. He may miss an opportunity to win her to him and build a bond because of his understanding of her past and her problems.

A different frame might arise from discovering these factors:

- She was neglected by her father and then dropped by numerous boyfriends.
- She was raped while attending college.
- She was abused by her first husband.
- She desires to feel safe and connected but is unable to overcome fear and pain from the past.
- She loves her husband greatly and prays for his patience as she works through issues.
- She longs to be asked about her feelings rather than be judged because of them.

- She wants nothing more than to be the focus of her husband's fantasies.
- She senses she is making progress toward a day of fully enjoying sex and the deep connection that can be felt through it.

If you take these elements and place them in the frame, you feel totally differently about the so-called frigid wife. Most frigid wives have these kinds of components in their lives. If we get behind the symptom causing the problem, we can discover the whole truth that led to the symptom. If we want to and are motivated to, because we care about this person, we can become an aid to healing and understanding rather than someone who inflicts more pain upon someone dealing with an inner conflict and deep wound.

The Impotent Husband

One of the greatest insults you can use with a man is to say he is sexually dead. It is an indictment on all of who he is, even though it is focused on one part of him. It implies weakness, inadequacy, and inability to perform as a man and fulfill his woman's desires. In marriage it is often viewed as a complete withdrawal from the relationship. The man who is judged sexually dead is assumed to have no interest in women or at least in his partner. In comparison to other men, especially those hyped up in the media, the man who is sexually dead is no man at all.

If you are married to a sexually dead husband and you nag or beg him, there is a good chance you are just shoveling more earth on top of his sexual deadness. You may be driving him deeper underground. Demands and labels are an easy default when it comes to a man who has lost his sex drive or at least put it in neutral. If you frame inside the labels, you dehumanize him and can more easily distance yourself from him and whatever has brought him to this place. But if we seek to live in full truth and make wise decisions, we need to look deeper and consider all the factors that may have led to his dilemma.

One of the most common causes I see is a man who uses pornography, saturating his mind with women who are beyond perfection and unflawed proportions. If he has done this for years, women have become objects to him. They are a collection of body parts that either please his jaded eye or they do not. If he is used to the beauty of a perfect twenty-one-year-old body with a flawless face, his marital sexual life will do nothing but go further and further downhill. The further away his wife gets from that ideal, objectified image, the less attractive she will be to him. Eventually she will not just be less attractive, she will become repulsive to him, and he will not want to have anything to do with her.

You can blame the impotent husband for his problem and judge him harshly, or you could also see him from another perspective. When he was growing up, no one knew how much pornography would proliferate and how many sexually stimulating images would be everywhere, from billboards to television to telephones to, well, everywhere. It is pretty easy to get addicted to the stuff if you don't have any tools with which to defend yourself. Today, when a man opens his computer and goes online, pop-up ads beg him to indulge himself. They can be nearly impossible to resist. Some check them out to satisfy their curiosity and find they can never be satisfied again. More than enough is never enough. And even if a man decides never to use it again, there will be a daily battle as the purveyors of porn invade his space and try to lure him back.

Recovering alcoholics most likely have never gone to work and had someone offer them a glass of vodka. But every day men are offered another look at a sexually explicit image. Is it his fault that he got caught up in this? Absolutely. But if we look at the total picture, we may have some compassion on him that moves us toward helping him rather than just judging or badgering him.

Seldom have I seen a man like this be able to radically change his behavior on his own. He needs to break through denial, shame, and isolation and ask for help. That help could consist of several things:

- Attending an Every Man's Battle workshop
- Attending Celebrate Recovery in a nearby church
- Finding a Sexaholics Anonymous meeting
- Joining an accountability group where other men know all about his problem and help him have victory over it

If a wife is willing to work with him when he is finally ready to get some help, he can retrain his brain, and they can one day resume a satisfying sex life.

But this is just one of many reasons this man might be sexually dead. Here are some others that might help us reframe the situation:

- He could be experiencing clinical depression and does not know he has it or how it needs to be treated.
- He could be suffering from an anxiety disorder that creates performance anxiety that results in impotence.

- He could be an undiagnosed diabetic.
- He could be suffering some nerve damage that prevents him from responding normally sexually.
- Some medication he is taking may be creating little or no libido and impotence.
- He may be too insecure to reach out for help from anyone.

These are just a few of a lot of different problems that humanize this man and make me want to help him. Even if infidelity or a lack of sexual integrity led to his problem, I don't want to abandon him. I don't want to give up on the two becoming sexually active again. I want to see healing no matter how they have reached this point.

His wife may be so angry and feel so much rejection that she may not be at that same place. If she can get some help in reframing her situation, reframing him, and reframing the future they could have together, there might be some hope for a satisfying marriage. She may not want to acknowledge this, but her husband has left her for any number of reasons and if they are going to be together, she is most likely going to have to make the first move to invite him safely back into the relationship. Then she will have to give him time to work out whatever it was that led to sexual deadness.

That whole process is what reframing is all about. It is the opposite of judging and rejecting just because the other person is doing or has done something terribly wrong.

Choosing a Creative Response

When you reframe your life, you live with a new level of discernment because you are always looking below the surface for more information before you make assumptions about people and situations. You develop keen insight that helps you in almost every area of your life and causes people to admire your ability to see what others overlook. You reach out to those who have hurt you because you have been able to review the times you have hurt others and you are aware of your ability to inflict pain. You live authentically within that truth about yourself. You acknowledge reality rather than deny it.

The reframed life is not confined to the past, but instead, past experiences are understood in ways that help you forge a future with expanded effectiveness because you have discontinued hurtful patterns and live free of resentment and bitterness. All of these elements are part of the reframed life.

There is more to reframing your life than greater knowledge, understanding, and wisdom. The person who wants a reframed life does not sit by and wait for the response of others. Instead, he can develop wisdom to develop a creative response leading to problem resolution and stronger relationships. Reframing is the end of waiting for someone else to take the lead in your life. You take the lead and actively, creatively, and productively choose a response to whatever area of your life is giving you difficulty. You move out actively to master the difficulties of life rather than be victimized by them.

Prison or Picnic

One lady was deeply troubled by very realistic nightmares she could not shake during the day. This emotional hangover interfered with work and friends, and she began to look like a panic-struck, deeply neurotic person. And it was all because of a theme running through each of these horrible dreams. In each dream she found herself in a dark prison with men who wanted to sexually assault her. It was worse than she imagined hell would be. In this prison, she was at the mercy of those men. The whole scene was dark and scary, and she had absolutely no control and no freedom.

It was no surprise this woman was quite controlling during the day. In her real world when the sun was up, she was the ultimate perfectionist holding everyone to a standard no one could meet. She was tough at work, and no one wanted to cross her. She demanded respect, but she knew those who worked for her were more fearful than respectful.

The dreams were all of her worst fears fulfilled. Of course this did not come out of nowhere. It came from her childhood and feelings about her father. The men in the dreams who wanted sex did not represent her father, but the feelings of being at the mercy of someone else did.

This woman's father never molested her. He was a moral man who loved his family very much. But he was not a good decision maker, nor was he a good businessperson. They lived comfortably in her early childhood, but eventually her father lost everything. When they moved into a cramped trailer, she felt great loss. She felt as if she should be able to make it all better, but things just got worse and worse and she was at the mercy of a man who did not know how to take control. So she promised herself she would never be in that situation again. She took control of her life and managed it and everyone else around her.

Seeing all this in counseling helped her immensely. She saw the need for letting go of many things. She began to change her life as she saw she was just as trapped by the need for control as she would be if she lost all control. She had a willing heart and wanted to experience the second part of her life in a new way, so she made great changes and bravely faced her need for control.

But the prison nightmares continued. Not every night, but they were frequent enough for her to worry every night whether or not she would have one. It was not her therapist who suggested what she might do to experience a breakthrough. She was the one who crafted the creative idea that would free her from the prison nightmares.

She decided to humanize the most inhumane place of her nightmares, or in other words, she wanted to reframe the biggest fear of her life. She had never been in a prison, and her only knowledge of them was what she saw in movies. So she decided to visit one and see it from the inside out. Her therapist knew a social worker who worked at the state detention center a few miles away. Through the social worker, she was able to go there, take a tour, and have lunch. Her lunch was a picnic she prepared for herself and the social worker.

The tour was somewhat stressful, but it revealed a place where people were busy. They were working and had other things to do. They were under control and not running free with their clothes off as she saw in her dreams.

Because she did her homework and created the tour and picnic idea, the power of prisons was reduced by familiarity.

She hung the pictures from her picnic prominently above her desk so she could focus on them to master the prison fear. The nightmares began to fade very quickly and were soon gone for good. She had been creative in her solution of how to reframe the dreaded place and it paid off in reframing her life as well as her nightmares.

Showering away the Shame

Sometimes creativity and dramatic acts can help reframe the way people see each other, even in the aftermath of betrayal and infidelity. In one of the saddest situations I have been involved with, it took every ounce of creativity and humility to reframe a tragedy so a young married couple would have a chance to build a marriage. The betrayal was on the part of the female who had a history of sexual addiction. She was a Christian, but as some Christians do, before her divorce was final she began to sleep around with several men who provided her with financial support as long as she was sexually involved with them. They bought her cars and helped her with bills, and in return she met their sexual needs. Sex was not something reserved for marriage. She felt entitled to it, and it got her what she wanted.

A young man from church was not aware of all this, and he fell madly in love with her. He had been divorced also, but he was determined to save himself for his next wife if there was to be one. He even resisted her attempts to have sex because he wanted to honor God with his sexual behavior.

After a year of dating, they married in a church and then took a honeymoon where things did not go so well. The sex between the two of them was not as great for her as sex with the other men, so she experienced great disappointment. She felt entitled to a great sex life, and when she thought that would never happen, based on the performance during the honeymoon, her mind and heart began to wander. The day she returned from her honeymoon, she began to look for attention from other men. When one offered it, she ended up having sex in the backseat of the car her new husband gave her. Six months later, she confessed the affair to him.

Already prone to depression, he was hit hard by the confession. He was so deeply depressed he wondered if he could recover. He had admired this woman and thought of her as the first person who really loved him, only to discover she only loved herself. He believed her when she said he was everything to her, and now he knew she was the one who felt arrogantly entitled to sex whether single or married. His heart was so broken, there were days he could not talk. Taking a shower was a major life accomplishment for him.

He wanted to divorce her and start over with his life, but he knew that would not solve anything. He truly wanted to forgive her, but all he could see was one who played him for a fool. She took from another woman's husband what she thought she deserved, all the time laying the foundation for her own husband to live as a broken man. He knew he needed to forgive her, but he did not know how nor how to help her get her mind off her shame. Eventually he created an experience that would help him move on rather than hold a grudge and resent her or leave her.

The idea came after he was reading the story of Jesus washing the feet of his disciples. Jesus on his knees to these men who revealed their immaturity and would reveal their lack of loyalty was a picture he could not get out of his head.

He eventually realized that if it was good enough for Jesus, it was good enough for him.

He invited his wife into the bathroom for a shower. He turned the lights out, and they could barely see each other's silhouettes. Rather than a sexual feel, it seemed like a sacred time. He moved her under the warm shower and began to shampoo her hair.

Their eyes never met as he washed her from top to bottom. When he got to her sexual parts, they both began to cry. He continued to wash her, working his way down to her feet. Slowly he washed her feet and rinsed them as he had the rest of her body. When he finished, they faced each other in the dark and hugged as they both burst into tears.

His act of love reframed her in cleanness and forgiveness, and it freed both of them to do the work needed to keep the relationship together. By anyone's standards, he was entitled to divorce her, but he really did love her and wanted to move beyond this major bump in the road. His creativity and sense of the dramatic started the process of healing that was difficult for both of them. The shower cleansing was part of a solution that saved their marriage. It did not do all the work, but it did provide a new frame in which he viewed his wife and she could view herself.

The dramatic act of a man washing and cleansing his wife was symbolic of what he wanted for her and for their marriage. This symbolic act became an invaluable image in their desire to move forward. That symbolic act remained a vision of where he was going when he would one day see her as pure and clean again. For her, it was an image of what she wanted to feel, and it helped her deal with the shame she had brought upon herself and upon their marriage.

That is what reframing can do in the worst of circumstances: it can provide a vision of what can be while we work through the painful reality of what is. It can provide a point of hope at the point of greatest pain.

The Big First Step

Reframing your life is a big first step in moving on with your life rather than allowing your life to be influenced or controlled by anything hurtful or regretful. Taking this big first step can lead toward the resolution of some very big hurts from the past that are taking up far too much space in the present.

Reframing also allows you to release current conflicts and see them as a part of every relationship rather than a reason to bail out when you feel uncomfortable due to disagreements. When a person reframes current difficulties, he or she allows for a daily reframing of the future, reaching for purpose and meaning while moving forward in an imperfect, difficult, and often hurtful world.

A reframed life moves out of the daily rut of stagnation and darkness. It begins a process resulting in effective living today with hope for a meaningful future, full of worthwhile contributions that add meaning to the lives of others.

CHAPTER SEVEN

It's Not Always Easy

A Very Tough Look at Abuse

If you have been abused or molested by someone, this section is going to be hard to read. You may have your defenses up already. That is understandable. You have learned to defend and protect yourself because you have experienced times when no one else was willing to do it. Every time you start to read something suggesting that whoever did this to you is not completely evil and doesn't deserve to die, you reject the thoughts outright. This is because you have lived and relived the horror, and anyone who hasn't shouldn't suggest you could come to a different understanding or view. But right now I want to present a concept about molestors and abusers that puts them in two different categories.

Through the years I have talked to many men who at one time or another have molested someone. These men fell into two broad categories. One category was the man who thought he was entitled to have sex with anyone and anything he wanted.

This type of man is very sick, has no conscience, no sense of right or wrong, and no desire to change. These are very rare. They even convince themselves what they are doing is not all that bad or harmful to the victims, and the rest of the world just does not understand them. The degree of their detachment from reality is severe.

If you were molested by one of these people, you were molested by a person who could be called a freak of nature. Through physiological brain malfunction and improper nurturing and/or abuse as children, people developed who had no concept of anyone but themselves. These people are so sick that outside of a miracle of divine intervention, they will never have one ounce of insight into themselves, their problem, or what they have done to someone else. In a way, they have defended themselves from understanding how destructive they are, because if they truly grasped all the suffering they caused, it would be unbearable. In a very real way, they are emotionally and relationally retarded.

Sensing Evil

When I meet these people, I often sense the presence of evil. It is a strange feeling, but it is real. Something is very different when I am in their presence. It makes me wonder every time if these people are evil or are the result of evil. Either way, the path to where they are was not all paved with flagrant choices to do evil. There were many influences from their pasts, from their wiring, and even from the addictive nature of some of the things they did.

While these persons will never seek forgiveness, they do deserve some level of forgiveness. They are so far down into the sickness, they have little if any ability to help themselves. Praying for a divine intervention is about all anyone can do.

If abused persons can reframe the evil done to them from this perspective, it helps in some ways to depersonalize what happened. They can see they were unfortunately within close proximity and vulnerable to very sick people. It was not the result of something the victims did or in any way a punishment or some other kind of act directed by God. It also had nothing to do with any kind of personality traits, characteristics, or faults of the victims. It was all about the unfortunate reality that on this earth we sometimes come face-to-face with evil people, and their problems become ours.

Seeing someone in this light does not complete the healing process, but it can initiate it. Reframing might be the perspective that opens the door to healing. It could be a giant step back from expecting the abuser to wake up to what he did and seek forgiveness. So often our grudges are attached to an expectation from the one who has offended us, and those expectations will most likely not be fulfilled. If you were abused, part of the healing is seeing what really was behind the abuse. It is also giving up any expectation of amends or reconciliation. It is reframing the act from something very personal to something that happens in a fallen world because evil and freedom of choice exist, and both of these may come together to hurt you.

The Remorseful Abuser

One night I was speaking on God's desire to forgive the worst of evils so he can have a relationship with those he loves so deeply. God is love, and he has done many things to remove the barriers that prevent or destroy a love relationship between him and us. I spoke of those who deserve his forgiveness because the unimaginable sacrifice on the cross covered all sins.

Jesus went to the depths of painful hell because he knew how horrific our sins were. He did not draw a line and say his sacrifice would cover only so much. He died so it all could be forgiven if we were willing to accept his sacrifice. I mentioned that even the rapist in prison was deserving of this forgiveness that comes out of the love of God and the sacrifice of his son.

When I was finished with my talk, a very fine and successful-looking man approached me and asked if he could have a couple of minutes. When we sat down, he told me how he got involved with a younger woman—fifteen when he was twenty-one and substitute teaching. He said the girl was very mature, expressed feelings for him, and he was not strong enough to resist the forbidden temptation. He had sex with her, she told her parents, and he went to prison for statutory rape. His punishment fit his crime. While in prison, he dedicated his life to Christ through the work of Prison Fellowship. Working with them, he was able to accept full responsibility for what he did, grieve for the fifteen-year-old girl, ask her and her parents' forgiveness, and accept Jesus as his Savior.

He wanted me to know that when I spoke of someone in prison who was the worst of the worst but entitled to experience the best of what God has, he said it spoke directly to him. He did what many would think unforgiveable but also experienced the Lord's miraculous forgiveness and moved on with his life, never coming close to repeating the offense.

He wanted me to know that when I talked about that in the

future, I would be describing real people who have made their way back, regretful of the past and unwilling ever to go through it again. This man falls into the second category of abuser, the one who has a conscience and can learn to care deeply for others.

This man represented all the other abusers who knew the depravity in which they were involved. In speaking with these strugglers, I have always found them to be full of shame over their deeds. They are wracked with pain and sorrow, often wanting to die rather than repeat what they have done. They wanted to be great fathers and ended up committing the worst sins. They are alone in their suffering because no one would understand, and they expect rejection.

Each time a lustful thought arises, they fight acting out but have nothing in place to prevent them from doing it. Their actions are both compulsive and impulsive. I have never met one of these abusers who was not in the deepest of miseries over the abuse of someone. They go from craving the perverted thrill to hating themselves after they have experienced it. Then they find all sorts of ways to cope with their split lives.

My point is they do not celebrate the fact they are hurting someone else. They are not proud of what they do. They are filled with shame—shame so great they are driven back to the thing they hate because it is the only thing they know to do to survive.

If you think that your abuser loved every minute of abusing you, you are most likely mistaken. It may be helpful to reframe him in a more realistic light. It may be time to give up the belief he was all evil and begin to believe there were some good things about this person. The abuser probably did not just come up with how to abuse you either. In some way this was history repeating itself and could have started generations ago.

This look at the abuser and the past is in no way an attempt to normalize or excuse what happened. It is taking a giant leap to understand there were many factors intertwined in this sick part of your history. And as horrific as it was to you, the abuser has probably also suffered with the shock, guilt, and shame of what he did.

Something's Gotta Give

So how does this help the innocent child who is still struggling with what happened—whether it was sexual abuse or something else—even as she enters her forties? If this is still a struggle, a major painful part of most days, then something needs to change. Something needs to be different. "Something's Gotta Give" is the title of an old song that expresses the reality for someone who is trapped in the past of abuse or neglect. You have not found the freedom or release from this horrific event that most people can experience even in the worst cases of abuse. So rather than stay stuck in old thoughts, I am suggesting you try on some new thoughts and new feelings. They could get you started down a new path with the knowledge of your past life still there, but the negative impact of it wiped out.

As I mentioned earlier, this does not solve anything, but it leads you to the next step of resolving. It is the beginning, not the end. And if this can help a person who has experienced cruel abuse as a child, it can help others who have suffered milder forms of mistreatment.

As we all know, when it is your pain from your experience,

you don't really care where it falls on the continuum of severity. It is yours and it hurts and it is real. So you could be experiencing the results in a very similar way a sexually abused child might, even though what happened to you was much different. So you too have to go through the painful process of seeing the abuser in a different light if you are to move on and begin the process of healing. The reframe job that needs to occur for you will be painful, but it will lead you to freedom, no matter the source of your pain. Especially if you have been stuck for years.

Giving Up the Old Frame

Since doing what you have been doing has not allowed you to move along, it is time to do something different. The first thing is to become willing to give up the old frame in which you have viewed this person. Here are some components you might have used in creating the frame around the picture you have carried around with you:

- The person is all bad.
- The person has no regrets.
- The person is beyond redemption.
- The person deserves nothing.
- The person has nothing of value to offer this world.
- The person is hopeless.
- The person should say he or she is sorry before I move on.
- The person is responsible for all [or almost all] my misery.

Any of these feelings or thoughts could be part of the frame you have put around this person. You can keep the frame firmly in place, but if you do, you will also keep your life right where it is. Give up your old frame, or at least be willing to look at some other things that could make up that frame, and you may be able to take that first step toward finally getting over it and getting on with your life.

In my own life, I have been betrayed in the worst of ways as an adult. Unfaithfulness and infidelity set me back in every area of my life. There seemed to be little or no remorse in the wake of it all. I told some people the other day that in the beginning, I wanted death for the person. Then I knew I was making progress when I only wanted the person to experience a chronic illness. Further progress was noted when I just thought a hemorrhoid or an inconveniently placed boil would satisfy me. But something began to happen.

First, I began to see that just because I had not committed a betrayal, I was not morally superior. Suffering betrayal did not provide a stepladder to a pedestal where I was entitled to point the finger for the rest of my life. I had to come down off that pedestal, and when I did, things began to change. I went from wanting the worst to not really caring what happened. And then, within a few years, I was at a place where I could say that I wanted good things for this person, not bad. So I have had to go through this reframing process of giving up the old materials of the frame and picking up some new ones so I could pick up my life and move on.

The First Piece of the Right Frame

The first piece of the right frame is made up of your own personal stance of humility. Like me, you may have crawled up on a moral pedestal and thought you were entitled to finger-pointing. But I think most of us eventually get back to the reality that is shared in Romans 3:23:

> For all have sinned; all fall short of God's glorious standard.

Every one of us has messed up, and we are all fellow strugglers. When we acknowledge this, we take away our entitlement to blame and shame. We take a little focus off the evil done to us and put a bit more emphasis on the reality of today and our current struggles as fallible human beings. We realize we would have made mistakes had no one hurt us. We would have had other problems if we had not had this one. Without this hurt, life still would not have been a piece of cake because we, in and of ourselves, would have sinned and made mistakes and fallen short and messed it up in other ways. Other people would have stepped in and hurt us in other ways. In other words, all of our lives and all of our pain cannot be blamed on someone who neglected, abused, and hurt us. We must humbly see ourselves as we really are.

The Second Piece

The second piece of the new frame is based on a concept found in Galatians 5:16. Here we are instructed to do exactly the opposite of what feels most normal.

So I advise you to live according to your new life in the Holy Spirit. Then you won't be doing what your sinful nature craves.

Those of us who have been hurt crave revenge. Our flesh and our instincts tell us to get even and ensure the other person is punished as harshly as possible. If we were animals or controlled by emotion and instinct, that is exactly what would happen. We would focus on all that would please us and all that would satisfy our longings for vengeance.

But we have a power we can tap into. We have a way of life we can experience where our base desires do not have to be played out. We can overrule them in living by a power greater than ourselves. It is important we find that power and lifestyle because our pain was a result of someone else's not being willing to live that way. All the abusers did was satisfy their earthly desires. So if we accomplish anything in this life, it should be to treat people better than our abusers did. The power of the Holy Spirit allows us to do that.

Life in the Spirit

I am not an expert in explaining the Holy Trinity, but I am going to do my best so this concept is not missed. Most everyone I know believes there is a supernatural God who allows us to do supernatural things. If you have ever prayed, you have believed in a supernatural God alongside perhaps three billion others or so praying at that exact moment. Only a supernatural God could hear all those prayers at once, and if you did not think God could, you would not have prayed. Second, you believed he could hear your prayer and actually do something about your request. Otherwise you would have thought of other options. You would have longed for outcomes, but you would not have asked God for the outcome you preferred the most. So most everyone believes in a supernatural God.

That supernatural God is so supernatural he exists in three forms but is still the same God. A poor comparison of this is the fact that I am a father, a husband, and a man all at the same time. I think and do things differently when I am acting as an independent man versus when I am acting as a husband or a father. This is how I think of the Trinity. Jesus was the Son of God who came to die for us and save us from our sins. It was God putting on an "earth suit" and coming down here to show us how to live and who God is. Then there is God the Creator, sitting on a throne, ruling the universe today as he did yesterday and as he will tomorrow. Then there is the dimension of God within us who is the Holy Spirit. The Holy Spirit empowers us to do what no one could do without supernatural intervention.

After reading a book by Bill Bright on the Holy Spirit, I began to call upon the Holy Spirit before I wrote or spoke or went into a meeting. I noticed a marked change in the outcomes of those situations. I felt the Holy Spirit responded to my request and whatever the outcome of the meeting, I was okay with it because I knew God had guided my thoughts and given power and wisdom.

As I ask for the presence of the Holy Spirit more and more, I can begin to walk by the Spirit. That means rather than react to anything done to me, I can maintain my composure, let some time pass, and then respond in a more loving way. I can let go of things others would hold on to. I can get beyond temptations because I am not living like others who are tied to the lusts and passions of their hearts. I am tied to my soul, which longs to please God and not fulfill earthly desires, but rather act out of an eternal perspective.

When I incorporate humility with living according to my new life in the Holy Spirit, a bit of bitter concrete starts to break off. I don't need the walls that protect me because I am walking in supernatural power with humility. I am not focused so much on the bad that has happened to me but am starting to look for what might be ahead. I start to see the person who hurt me as one who needs what I have, and I may begin praying for the healing of that other person.

When I do that, I have replaced the earthly desire for revenge with a spiritual lifestyle in no need of revenge. The next time you are tempted to become enraged, remind yourself you have a power within that can conquer anything.

The Third Framing Piece

The third piece of framing is simply an awareness of or an acknowledgment that the person who hurt you was raised in a broken world and was most likely abused, abandoned, or hurt in some way that led to his or her sickness. You could call this simply being aware of the reality of the imperfect life.

You live in it, and you live in it imperfectly. You, just like everyone else, have done some hurtful things to others. You are part of imperfect humanity. You share a bond of imperfection that comes out of God's gift of free choice. That gift has freed you to make up your own mind and choose your own priorities. In living with free will, all of us have made poor choices and hurt others, and most of us have been hurt by the poor choices others have made.

This is a key piece of framework because when we have been brutally abused or sinned against, the temptation is to see ourselves as all good and that other person as all bad. In the moment, seeing the person that way helps us to survive. But we can eventually come to see that person as something other than all bad and ourselves as all good. We can integrate the good and the bad as we reframe our lives. We can move on without being victimized over and over again by focusing on a person who is no longer in our lives or some event we can do nothing to change.

We all make mistakes of our own free will. The mistakes made against you were choices someone had to make. But that person probably did not have a lot of support to make healthy choices. There is a real live Satan who influences us in subtle ways, leading us off course. There is peer pressure, which often takes us down the wrong path, not making the choice for us, but leading us right up to it. The media sickly portrays every kind of perversion and pleasure, making us feel incomplete if we don't indulge ourselves in any and every-thing we desire.

All of these influences, along with a less-than-perfect childhood—and perhaps a childhood influenced by evil—has led you to being hurt. If you can see it in a context of a very evil world, and see the abuser as having succumbed to that context but still possessing some level of good within, it may help you reframe him and the event and lead you toward re-solving your past.

The Fourth Framing Piece

The fourth framing piece is a mind-set providing you with a new way of looking at the past and those who hurt you, but it will also allow you to connect with those in the present who continue to inflict pain and stir up trouble in your life. It is not the actual act of forgiveness, but it is having a forgiving spirit.

This spirit or way of approaching all of life is a way to live with much less conflict and emotional turmoil. If you have ever seen someone in the midst of road rage, or perhaps you have acted impulsively in the midst of road rage, you know firsthand what it is like not to live like this. Being willing to embarrass yourself by stopping another car to confront someone about his or her horrible driving reveals someone full of anger, who lives on the edge of indicting everyone. That is a very hard life.

If you have a forgiving mind-set, you expect that people are going to slight you. In any given day, you are going to have to forgive many slights, insults, and unintentional hurts. In this grace-filled way of life, you are daily ignoring the personal mistakes of others, and you are making an effort to see every good thing that happens to you as a gift.

You start to say to yourself, "I can get over that." "I am going to let that go." "I can just turn that over." You develop an attitude of forgiveness and grace that makes you easy to live with, and it makes it easy for you to live inside your own skin.

In a sense, you stop personalizing everything unpleasant that happens to you and begin to see the people behind the hurtful events. The poor service at the restaurant has a lot less to do with you than the bad situation the server is experiencing at home. The guy who cuts you off in traffic may be late for his job for the last time before getting fired. His poor "traffeticut" may have nothing to do with his wanting to hog the road or bulldoze you off it. He might just be trying to survive and save his job.

If you start thinking like this, when the deeper hurts of life come along or linger, you tend to see them in a less-personal way. You come to understand that you were abused because you were in the proximity of the person, not because you are a sitting duck for abuse or were a target from the time you were born.

This is a reframed attitude that leads to the reframed life. You are more forgiving, less personalizing, and more others-centered in this fourth valuable framing piece.

Putting It All Together

When you put it all together, the reframed life is a combination of humility, awareness, spiritual focus, and grace. These four components can help you reframe anything from the past or in the present. They can even help you move toward a bright future.

In *humility* you find many equals with whom to connect. You resist the temptation to see yourself as better than someone else. Jesus lived in humility. To walk like him, sometimes you will need to take a step back and allow someone to walk ahead. You will allow for others and look after them, and you will stop worrying so much about yourself, how you look, and what others think.

With this humble heart, you will be living like Jesus and placing the priority on the spiritual rather than physical comforts or emotional traumas. You will live in the spiritual realm, tapping into a spiritual perspective that leaves you connected to others who are drawn to you.

In *awareness* you do not ignore what others might. You realize we are all in this together, and you find ways to connect rather than declare superior breeding.

Accepting the imperfections of life rather than holding on to an idealized view of life that will always let you down is a sign you have a new *spiritual focus* on your own and others' imperfections.

With this mind-set, you are able to move from reframing to *resolving grace*.

When you put the four pieces of the frame together, then put them around even the vilest abuse, you become open to resolving it and putting it behind you. If you have been holding on to the same grudge, resentments, or bitterness for years, it is time to let those go and live your life from a different perspective. That perspective can lead you to resolution and never having to relive the pain—or ever allow the abuser to influence or control your life—again. Once you achieve this, you are free to move into the future and live out the purposes God created for you to accomplish.

CHAPTER EIGHT

Reframing Right Now

Hey! What Are You Looking At?

I think most people have caught someone staring or glaring at them and blurted out, "Hey! What are you looking at?" Once the rude person realizes his mistake, he quickly diverts his eyes. Our question is a challenge to someone who is focusing on us or something about us when we don't want the attention or the scrutiny.

It is a great phrase to use to get someone's attention. It is also a great way for us to get our own attention. It can help us wake up to the fact we may be looking at exactly the wrong thing, focusing on the wrong area, and we need to reframe the present circumstance or conflict.

So before we move on, let me ask you to think about your current situation. Think about the conflict that causes you the most problems. Think about the relationship that is not providing you with all you need or expect. Then ask yourself, "Hey! What are you looking at?" Chances are, you are looking at the wrong thing or the wrong person, and once you change that, the whole situation can be reframed in a way that might lead to resolution rather than repeated conflict and pain.

A Man's Right to Have Sex

The other day I received a phone call from a man who had an amazing ability to focus on the wrong thing. When it came to his wife and what she was doing wrong, he had twenty-twenty vision. But when it came to seeing where he was messing up, the man was completely blind. Until he could reframe his situation in light of his own mistakes and problems, he and his wife were going to move further and further apart.

His question to me revolved around his right to have sex with his wife. He was focused on a woman's biblical mandate not to withhold sex from her husband. He was sure he was 100 percent right about its being wrong for a woman not to have sexual relations with her husband unless they both agreed for a spiritual reason. He knew his "rights," and he wanted to know what he was entitled to do based on them.

It had been three months since he last had sex with his wife. For a man who wanted to have sex every day, that was a very long time. He pleaded with her to meet his need so he was not tempted to go out and have it met somewhere else. He even took out the Bible and showed her the passage where she was instructed by God to have sex with him. For three months he asked for and then demanded she perform her wifely duties for him, but she refused. It was as if she did not even care if the two of them ever had sex again.

His question was concerning time. He wanted to know

how much time he needed to give her before he was entitled to move on with his life: divorce her and find a wife who would have sex with him. He was ready to pull out of the relationship because, after all, she was going against what God wanted her to do in their marriage—have sex with him.

The Other Side of the Bed

Immediately I wondered what was going on in the relationship to drive this woman to the other side of the bed and adamantly refuse to be sexual with a man who wanted her. Rarely does a woman just up and decide one day she is finished with sex, has no place for it in her life, and informs her husband there will be no more where all the rest came from.

I asked him to stop a minute and reframe this entire situation from a different perspective. I asked him to step back, and to the best of his ability, slip over onto her side of the bed and see and feel the situation from her perspective. I asked him to, as honestly and openly as possible, reveal to me from her heart what she has been feeling the past couple of years that would lead her to this place of withholding sex.

After a bit of defending and resisting, he unfolded the story of their marriage and his own struggle with alcohol. I was amazed at how open and honest he was about his own failings once he took his sight off her and put the glare back on himself.

It turns out this sexually demanding man was an alcoholic who experienced five years of sobriety through attendance at Alcoholics Anonymous meetings and minimally working the program. Prior to involvement in that program, he had been arrested for driving under the influence. Forced into the program, he managed to put together many months of sober living.

When I asked him why he stopped, he said he started to feel as if he did not need it anymore. Then once he relapsed, he reembraced his right to drink.

He was honest enough to tell me his wife had not started out withholding sex. She started by suggesting things could not stay the same if he was not willing to get help. Then she refused sex when he was drinking. Then she said she was not going to be sexual with him until he got sober. At no point had he shown any interest in making any changes. What he had shown was great interest in the Bible passage that says a woman should not withhold sex from her husband.

Using Truth in Untruthful Ways

The Scripture he focused on to use to get his way is found in 1 Corinthians 7. It reads as follows:

> The husband should not deprive his wife of sexual intimacy, which is her right as a married woman, nor should the wife deprive her husband. The wife gives authority over her body to her husband, and the husband also gives authority over his body to his wife. So do not deprive each other of sexual relations. The only exception to this rule would be the agreement of both husband and wife to refrain from sexual intimacy for a limited time, so they can give themselves more completely to prayer. Afterward they should come together again so that Satan won't be able to tempt them because of their lack of self-control. (vv. 3–5)

He certainly had a biblical point to make. And there are all sorts of evidence of how husbands and wives have been lured away from each other when one spouse was not available.

He had a point, but it was not the ultimate point. It was not a point greater than his need to get help and stop drinking and become the man she hoped she married. In light of the larger dilemma from which he was unwilling to budge, he was using truth in an untruthful way. He was using it to manipulate her into compliance while avoiding responsibility for his own life and his own recovery.

In my opinion, he was a fallen leader of his tribe. He was a fallen husband who did not have the right to demand anything until he got his act together.

So I invited him to reframe his situation in a way I hoped would help move them out of the stalemate of each wanting something from the other that the other was not willing to give.

The Other Side of the Coin

I acknowledged his willingness to be up-front about his drinking problem and invited him to stop and see his situation differently. I wanted him to reframe on the spot. I presented a different passage of Scripture I thought was far more important than the one to which he clung. The passage is from the fifth chapter of Ephesians:

And you husbands must love your wives with the same love Christ showed the church. He gave up his life for her to make her holy and clean, washed by baptism and God's word. He did this to present her to himself as a glorious church without a spot or wrinkle or any other blemish. Instead, she will be holy and without fault. In the same way, husbands ought to love their wives as they love their own bodies. For a man is actually loving himself when he loves his wife. No one hates his own body but lovingly cares for it, just as Christ cares for his body, which is the church. And we are his body.

As the Scriptures say, "A man leaves his father and mother and is joined to his wife, and the two are united into one." This is a great mystery, but it is an illustration of the way Christ and the church are one. So again I say, each man must love his wife as he loves himself, and the wife must respect her husband. (vv. 25–33)

I pointed out that a man who refused to quit drinking yet demanded sex is not too easy to respect. I asked him to see his life as his wife saw it, showing some signs of great hope and then spiraling back down into drunkenness and misery. And rather than have a husband willing to work on it and honor her with his humility, he arrogantly demanded sex. He wanted a physical home run, but he had not even made it to first base emotionally.

I told him that in most cases like his, a woman would simply walk out the door or have an affair, but at least his wife was still with him, hoping one day he would love her so much that respect and admiration would again well up within her.

I told him he could waste a lot of time and a lot of money, but he could also reframe right now and see himself as the one needing to make a move. He could pick up a phone and find out where the next meeting was, then call his wife and tell her he would be home late because he was going to a meeting and getting his life back on track. I explained to him that if he made this move, I didn't think her willingness to have sex would be a problem any longer.

What About Your Right Now?

As you read about this fallen husband who could reframe right then and change everything, did you think of a situation you could reframe right now? Is there some person you have been holding out on who has your best interests in mind? Have you been resisting the suggestions of someone who really loves and cares for you? Have you twisted that person's requests for your best into attempts at control? Do you need to take a step backward and reframe the *right now* that you are living in?

It does not take months of therapy for you to see the other person's perspective. It does not take great insight developed over years or attending meetings to understand that if you will give up your right to stay sick or never forgive, you can reframe right now into a new beginning.

Before you move on, ask yourself if there is a point you are holding onto that is perhaps a point of truth, but it is not the ultimate point. Whatever it is you need to do, take a step and do it. Reframe right now so you will not be stuck in your problem for months or years to come.

CHAPTER NINE

Reframing Everyday Life

The reframing way of life can be a great help in making life easier and more manageable. Time can be spent more productively and stress can be lowered. I guess you could say it is a mini-health club because you are less angry, have lower blood pressure, and are less likely to get shot on the freeway. There is even another benefit: the real you has a chance to emerge when you don't need so many defenses to help you get by. If you are willing to try reframing, you can apply the principles to everyday situations that will become less and less of a challenge the more you incorporate reframing into them.

Traffic

Unless you live in the country, there is a good chance traffic has become an irritation to you from time to time. It seems most of us who live in big cities or the suburbs surrounding them are often stuck in traffic due to the poor planning of the city's leaders. It seems that just as the construction ends on a major road, they have to start again because the traffic is so much heavier than they planned for. If you are someone who lets traffic get to you, you could end up having five workdays' worth of irritability and frustration. A little reframing could change all that.

Reframing the traffic jam requires allocating time for it. Rather than always being inconvenienced by it because you did not plan on its happening, plan to be in a traffic jam and allocate additional time for it. If it does not happen, you will either arrive early or have time to go and get your day started with a real breakfast.

The beginning of getting out of traffic "hell" is believing it will happen ahead of time and being pleasantly surprised when it does not. Removing the time pressure takes care of most of the downside of traffic jams unless you operate a car that is prone to heating up when it can't stay in motion.

Once you have allocated time for your own personal traffic jam, you can reframe the time you spend alone in your car. Rather than be frustrated with not moving very fast, plan ahead for those precious moments you have to yourself. Go to the trouble of buying your favorite music online or on CD. Pick music you love so much you hate for the ride to end.

I do more than listen. I bought some karaoke tracks of songs from the forties and fifties, and I sing along and learn the words while I wait. It is a great time for goal setting and jotting down ideas that might have a future. The longer you are stuck, the more phone calls you can return, freeing up your time the rest of the day. If you can reframe this frequent inconvenience and make plans for it, traffic jams may become the favorite part of your workweek.

Teaching Kids to See Things Differently

If you have kids, this is not just your "right now," it's theirs too. You can model reframing for them, and you can teach them how to reframe almost anything, especially the tough aspects of their lives. A mother was upset because the family was going to move due to the husband's new job. None of the kids wanted to move because they had done so many times before. They just wanted to stay put, but it was not an option. The mother wondered if she would lose her close relationships with them. Instead of losing them, she decided to connect with them in a different way.

She called a family meeting and passed out pieces of paper. She had them answer some questions about the move. She asked them to write down the worst thing about moving. She asked for the horrible feelings the first day of school in a new place. She asked them to write down how they felt about their father, who was forcing them to move. She wanted to know what she could tell him to make him understand how badly they needed to stay. She wanted to know some threats they wanted communicated to him—these were things they might do if they were forced to move. She asked them to write down the worst part about being their father's children. She asked them to write out what they would do if they were parents and their own family did not want to move. She had each one take the time to write out the details of his or her feelings.

You can imagine what happened. One by one, they began to see things from their father's perspective. Rather than want to hurt him, they started to defend him to each other. When one read a complaint, another chimed in, but someone else took up for good old Dad. Before long, they reframed their situation from his perspective, and although they did not want to move, and she acknowledged those feelings as real and okay, they supported their father's need to move to provide for them.

She took the reframing exercise one step further. She asked them to think about how these moves were going to benefit them later in life. They came up with many different strengths, such as the ability to adjust to uncomfortable situations and the differences between people. They talked of their sense of adventure and how the world seemed smaller to them than it did to friends who never moved. They benefited from knowing so many different people and making new sets of friends in each place.

The wise mother was unwilling to let the move disconnect her and her husband from her kids. She helped them reframe the move and that reframed her relationship with them and their relationship with their father.

A Perfect Day Spent Inside

I love to kayak on a lake, river, or the ocean. Put a paddle in my hand and my bottom in a kayak and I am most likely going to be in the best frame of mind possible. The other day was a perfect day, and I was looking forward to my buddy and me being out on the ocean together in our kayaks. There is not much of a better time than right there at the surface of the ocean, with whales and dolphins and sea lions that might pop up for a visit at any time.

But on this perfect day he had to go be with his family, do the responsible thing and be there for them, rather than have some fun with me out in the kayaks. I was really bummed. I needed to reframe my *right now*.

I had a choice: to mope about my lost opportunity or to make the most of a bad situation. I knew it would be better if I just stayed put for the day and caught up on things I had been letting slide. So the two hours I would have been out on the ocean blue I devoted myself to catching up on things at home. When I was done, I felt so great there is no way two hours on the ocean could have compared. Doing the dreaded things I had put off turned out to be one of the best gifts I had ever given myself. It happened because I was able to reframe a disappointment into an opportunity.

You can do that in your own life over and over again. The worst day can always be a perfect day if you will find the opportunity after you have grieved a bit over the disappointment. The tough job you have could be an opportunity to go back to school and get a degree or specialized training so you never have to have another crummy job. The painful firing you endured is an opportunity to find something you love doing and do so well you would never face firing again. The child in trouble with drugs or sex provides you with an opportunity to love him or her the way God loves you. It is an opportunity to stretch yourself to show love he or she may not know exists. Every disappointment we face can be reframed into an opportunity if we will practice doing it so much that it becomes a natural reaction to anything unpleasant in life.

Avoiding Mr. Wrong

A very good friend of ours was dating one of the best-looking men I have seen. He could have been on the cover of a men's fashion magazine. The two of them looked like Barbie and Ken, only more human. They dated and moved closer and closer

together until finally they were engaged. Everything was rock-
ing along as expected until she picked up a book I wrote called
Avoiding Mr. Wrong. In that book it described "Mr. Wonderful." Mr. Wonderful looks too good to be true because that is
exactly what he is. He does not do great things out of love, he
does them out of a desire to manipulate and control. He is a
narcissist who thinks he owns the world and the world should
revolve around him.

This was the kind of guy she was attracted to over and over
again. And it always ended up in the same place: both of them
in love with the same person—him. But as she read about Mr.
Wrong, some lights began to come on, and she saw who he
really was below all the overboard displays of mannerly consideration and treatment. She detected his short fuse and the lies
under which he lived. Her radar would have never detected
that under the bright smile and perfectly pressed clothes was
a man who wanted, needed, and demanded control of the
relationship.

She saw who he was, and she saw why she would be attracted to him. She reframed him from the great-looking guy
on the outside to a more accurate view of a very controlling
and manipulating man on the inside. She broke up with him
and set out to meet as many people as possible.

She joined two dating services, and both of them worked. In
one of her matches she went out with a guy who had a brother.
Her date thought his brother would be much more appropriate for her than he. He was right, and they fell in love. I had
the privilege of marrying them. In the ceremony I was pleased
to announce to the audience, "What God and Match.com have
put together, let no man put asunder."

I have never seen so many people happy for a couple as

they were for this one. This marriage would have never happened if she had not been willing to take a second look at her fiancé and make the bold move of breaking up and becoming open to whatever God had to offer.

Daily Opportunities at Reframing

Today will have opportunities for reframing, and if you take yourself up on those opportunities you can enjoy your life so much more. The dreadful breakup is reframed as an opportunity for new adventures, new hobbies, and new friends. It is no longer the end of the world, it is just a transition into some exciting new things previously ignored.

And reframing allows you to break up with a lot of people who have been living in your head. You can usher them out of your thoughts and free them to move on as you move on beyond them.

You can also reframe the bad people in your life from being all bad to being a combination of good and bad. Focusing on the good can take the power out of the crummy things all of us have to some degree.

Rather than judging a person's inadequacies, you can follow the example of my friends Milan and Kay Yerkovich, the authors of *How We Love*. They practice and teach others to get a "PhD" in each other's wounds. When you begin doing that, you have transitioned fully out of yourself and into others in a reframed life.

CHAPTER TEN

Reframe Your Life Rather Than Retreat from It

I have known people who pick up a book as a last effort to find something to hang on to before they give up. I want to take a few pages to address this point of despair for those who might be experiencing it. It is a dark place when you don't know if you have what it takes to just hang on for one more day, especially when so many hurts have piled up around you, and you feel hopeless about ever returning to a normal life. The losses may be too great for you to imagine any kind of enjoyable life. You may see everything in a very dark frame.

If so, I want you to know I have been there. I know the depths of the pain and the emptiness and feelings of futility in life. Fortunately I have lived through it, that horrible "valley of weeping," and come out on the other side. You can too if you will allow God to help you. I'd like to share what happened to me. I hope within the story you find some insights that help you hang on for today so you can move on with hope and promise for a new life.

The Frame of the Dark Side of Life

I remember, a few years back, thinking my life was too easy. I was making a comfortable salary, writing a lot of books, running Women of Faith, which had reached more than three hundred thousand a year in attendance, and working with New Life Ministries, which had ample funds to do whatever we felt God leading us to do. I remember thinking it could not last. I knew God loved me and would not allow me to stagnate in comfort. There had to be some challenges and changes up ahead. Boy, were there ever.

When my ex-wife filed for divorce, the frame around my own life became about as dark and deathly as it could be. I was stretched to the depths of my faith, living day to day with the reality of a betrayal and then divorce. It was hard to imagine continuing with my life. I did not think I would continue to do workshops and seminars. I thought speaking was out of the question, and I felt my calling as an author had come to an end. I knew I could still write books, but I did not think publishers would be interested as they were before. Previously, I was able to get any book published I wanted. Now, I thought that would all change.

I thought my relationship with my daughter, Madeline, would radically change. So often a young girl will hold the father responsible for the divorce—not because he caused it, but because he should have prevented it. We did so much together and had built a rare bond, but I felt it was all over.

I was living in a dark cloud that framed all my decisions and interactions with others. I lived there inside that frame for many months.

The frame began to surround a dark picture of the future. I envisioned myself as a lonely bachelor, sitting in the front room staring out at the ocean with no stress, no pressure, and nothing really important to do. I saw myself as a man old for his age, just serenely getting by in a lonely house with very little connection with others. It was a dim picture, and the frame I put around it all was one of disappointment, despair, darkness, and death. It was a sorry way to view life in the future.

The Frame of Life

Fortunately, I began to emerge from the darkness. All-bad days were replaced with a pretty good one every now and then. The world began to open up, and I started to wake up to a couple of pieces of reality that were helpful. One was that I was not dead, nor was I going to die anytime soon. Another one was that the future was going to be created by things I could control and things I could not. So, I had better do the best I could with the things I could actually control.

Life started to come back. I began to see the future with light and life rather than all darkness and dread. The words *potential* and *possibilities* started to pop into my head again. The passion for reaching out to others resurfaced. I was coming out of the depression, and the frame of my life started to change.

As I opened to new possibilities, things out of my control

started to happen that spurred me on to start dreaming again. All the negative things I suspected and predicted would happen did not. The radio audience I spoke to each day seemed to understand the circumstances and showed tremendous support. I think I received two negative e-mails. It was as if I had built a connection with our audience for this very time together. They understood there was no scandal on my part, just a tragedy I could not prevent. In fact, this horrible event drew us even closer. I had people contacting me telling me of new support they were giving for New Life and a new motivation to listen to the program. Rather than seeing our financial support hit a horrible slump, it went up. And I was off and running to see what I could do to build the radio ministry and other parts of New Life.

In publishing, I started receiving calls from people I had never worked with before and some I had not worked with in a long time, asking me to consider publishing a book about healing from the divorce. Several wanted to publish it, and they did not need to look at a manuscript, they just wanted me to agree to do it when I was ready and they would provide me an advance. After much consideration I agreed to publish it with Thomas Nelson and was given the largest advance I had ever received from a publisher.

So rather than publishing's being over, it opened up in bigger and more exciting ways, and last year I published *Healing Is a Choice* with Thomas Nelson. The results were beyond expectation. I was so thrilled to get the e-mails and letters from so many saying they had been helped by the book. Then other offers for other projects came in, and I am having the best days of writing now rather than that calling being over.

For a while I would not even talk to anyone of the opposite sex. Then I opened up a bit and started dating. Then I met Misty. She was full of life and meaning and laughter and love. She was like no one I had ever been with before. She framed our times with humor and joy and more and more laughter. It was hard for me to believe she would even be interested in someone like me. But she was, and the more we got to know each other, the more we saw a future together. No one even came close to capturing my heart the way she did. It was a miraculous time, full of life and love, and we decided to marry.

We had been married about nine months when we decided it was time to have a baby. You hear all these stories about women being radiant and beautiful when pregnant, and Misty really exceeded all expectations. It was a sweet time getting ready for this little boy we would name Solomon Russell Arterburn. On August 16, 2006, he was born. What an experience of life.

When the dust settled from the birth, I realized the frame of my life had completely changed. At one time it had all been about the dark side and every negative possibility. Now it was all about everything good and wonderful and full of life. New Life had a new life. Publishing had a new life. I was married to someone full of life. My relationship with Madeline gained new life, and the family gained a new life in Solomon. The frame went from lonely isolation and despair to life-giving and life-fulfilling choices and developments. What seemed to have been the end was just the beginning of something new and better and very different. The things I could and could not control all blended together to create a frame of hope and healing and life.

Give Up the Darkness

If you are living where I was living, in that darkest of places without hope and engulfed in pain, it is time to find a way out of that dreadful place. To get out, you have to give up all the things that make your world such a dark place. Don't allow treatment from others to determine how you treat yourself. Give up joining the people who want to pile on top of you. Don't magnify the mistakes you have made, telling yourself others don't make them and you can't get over them. Stop comparing yourself to others who have not been where you have been or had to overcome the same obstacles. Don't allow yourself to be bitter over unmet expectations. Allow yourself the freedom to live without any of those expectations being met. Set some new and more realistic expectations. Don't let the guilt and shame pile up inside. Don't let a single mistake or tragedy color your entire life. Refuse to be defined by your limitations and inadequacies.

You can reframe your life out of all these negative perspectives into a frame of perseverance where you hang on and hang around long enough to see what miracles can come out of your circumstances.

If you were around me very long, you would agree with me that I am nothing special. If God could allow me to build a new family full of life and love, he will do it for you as well.

You may feel as if you have to give up, that life is just too difficult for you. If that is the case, just don't let this be the day you give up. Choose to live for one more day. Call someone or talk to a friend or get involved in something that takes your mind off the losses that have brought you to this point.

Believe that joy comes in the morning. Live your life knowing the darker your life is today, the brighter it will shine if you will just not give up on this day. God has not given up on you—don't give up on him.

CHAPTER ELEVEN

Reframe Your God

Few people can reframe their lives without doing some reframing of their God. They have missed the identity of God and view God from a distorted perspective. They expect things from God he never promised. They project things onto God he might have allowed to happen but certainly did not cause. They have a different God than the God of the Bible, and if they want their lives to be better, they have to reframe God in an accurate light.

Born-Again Breakdown

Just last week I was talking to a man who, the year before, in a moment of desperation after tragedy upon tragedy piled up in his life, made the decision to turn his life over to Christ. He had messed up his life in many areas and actually believed he would destroy himself if he stayed on the same path. So he got involved with a church group that led him to the Lord, and everything in his life changed. They took him in, ministered to him, and made him feel he was part of their family. It was a natural step to accept the Christ they all believed in and worshiped.

Things were a little better for a while, but the feelings of euphoria began to wear off. Reality started to set in. And then his first disappointment as a Christian occurred. The relationship he was in fell apart. She wanted to be with someone else, and he could do nothing to stop her. The pain of losing her was secondary to the pain of waking up as a Christian and realizing that God was not going to make everything work out perfectly. The belief that life would get easier and more predictable after accepting Christ would not hold up under the reality of life.

When this man realized how badly things could still go, it shattered his new world, and he sank deeply into depression. He needed to reframe God accurately so he could develop a realistic relationship with him that would not depend on whether or not all of the man's desires were being met.

God Is Not an Air Bag

Can you imagine a world in which people count on their supernatural air bags to pop out before anything horrible happens? If you are about to drown, your air bag goes off and you quickly float to the surface. If a plane crashes, no worries because your air bag from God will deploy just before you hit the ground or are engulfed in flames. You can't get hit by a car and killed because you have that air bag working for you all the time. Thinking of life in this way seems absurd, yet many people expect this from God. They want a guarantee on a pain-free life that is exempt from struggle. Keeping God in this frame will never lead to intimacy and could lead to missing all God has for you because you are so focused on all God has not done for you.

God Is Not Your Overly Critical Parent

Some people keep God in the frame of an overly critical parent. Perhaps it was Dad who never seemed to feel you had performed well enough. Maybe in his mind, the more critical he was, the tougher he thought you would be. A father like this most likely did not have many positive feelings for anyone in his life, and his child had to suffer.

When you grow up like this, you always feel you are being judged and criticized by Christ. You feel the sting of a very long finger pointed at you, and there is a good chance you believe God feels just as Dad did. Until you resolve those conflicted feelings about your dad, they will taint your relationship with God. Reframing your relationship with Dad will impact the reframing of God.

God Is Not Your Detached Parent

If your parents—especially Dad—were not there, it will be difficult to believe that God is there for you. You may buy into a belief that God has placed the world in motion but does not have much to do with us. You may feel so distant you don't really believe God matters all that much. You have never had a close relationship with anyone greater than you, and because you have had to survive on your own, you developed a feeling of independence. God is just one of many people you cannot or will not connect with because your parents did not connect with you and nurture you in the way you needed.

You may have detached from God, but God has not detached from you.

The Moses Model and the Messiah Model

To you, Jesus might be a policeman either watching what you do or punishing you for what you did. He might be Santa Claus, there to provide you with everything you ever dreamed of. Everyone has a little different view of God, but I want to show you something that might help you discover who he really is.

First of all, there is the Moses model of God. In the Moses model, a big shot tells people what they need to do to get their acts together. He has a huge list of don'ts that, if disobeyed, will zap them in some way for not obeying him. If you are in a church with this model of ministry, you probably feel a lot of shame from those who do nothing more than give you the dos and don'ts, the rules and regulations. That is what I call "the Moses way of helping people."

When Jesus ministered, it was much different. He reframed just about everything. As I mentioned earlier in the book, he would use the phrase "You have heard it said," and then after giving one of those Moses-styled truths, Jesus said, "But I say." He would take the original law or concept and move it into the heart and reframe it in a more meaningful way.

He said that a lot of people focus on whether or not they are going to kill someone. And as long as they don't pull the trigger and end someone's life, they are feeling good about their compliance with the no-murder rule. But Jesus said you should be aware you may be harboring bitterness and anger and resentment, and those are just as ungodly as murder. So Jesus took the headline and went further and deeper with it so people would not think they had done some great work when in their hearts they are angry and bitter. They were shown that no matter what you do on the outside, it is the inside that matters most.

Jesus also did this about adultery. He said while a man may not have physical sex, he may still turn his head to look upon a woman lustfully. If you are lusting in your heart, it is pretty close to having sex with your body.

Jesus was frequently reframing the truth, and when he did, he challenged us to go deeper.

Who God Is

There are so many misconceptions about God, it is always good to reframe God according to who he was in the Bible. He was uncomplicated and he connected deeply. He was full of love, and he experienced the deep emotions many of us have been through. God is love. He shows us love in thousands of ways, and it is our job to look for them and celebrate the fact we are not too small or unimportant to be loved by God.

In the reframing process of your life, don't forget to reframe your image of God. It could help you live your life more connected to God and others. You'll enjoy a deeper faith in God because you know him for who he is.

CHAPTER TWELVE

From Reframing to Resolving

The Hard Stuff

Reframing is not an easy task, but when it becomes a lifestyle or a way of thinking, life becomes much more manageable. Reframing is a huge step to take. Many would rather hold on to their old view than reframe anything in a different light. Hopefully the pain of the trap they set for themselves will one day motivate them to get out and live a new kind of life.

The first step to new life is the reframing process. But reframing is not an end in itself. It merely leads to a deeper step of resolving the conflicts and difficulties built up over the years and could be piling up in the present. The resolving step is much more difficult and may take a lot more time, but it is where true healing takes place.

If you are familiar with other things I have written or been in a workshop I conduct, you know I do not believe in quick fixes and instant solutions. Quick fixes and instant solutions are really false hopes and temporary results. They make you feel a little better for a while, but they soon lead back into the place you were before. It is like life in a never-ending elevator ride. You push a button to get to the next floor. The bells and lights make you feel as if you are about to get off in a different place, but when you open the door you are on the same floor you thought you left. You have to do the work if you want to live your life above the place you are now.

Resolving is the work that follows reframing. It is the ongoing recovery of your life. The longer you are involved in resolving and recovering, the more insight you will develop, the more wisdom you will acquire, and the more comfortable you will live because you will have moved up and on to a better way of life.

The Ultimate Upgrade

Everybody likes an upgrade. I love it when I check into a hotel late at night, all the cheap rooms on the same floor as the Country and Western Line-Dancing Marathon are taken, and they have no choice but to upgrade me to a nice little suite on the same floor where there are complimentary snacks in the lounge down the hall.

One time my family took a trip to a resort called Atlantis. There were six of us, and the adjoining rooms we reserved at a greatly reduced price on the ground floor next to the parking lot were all taken. They had to put us on the top floor in a suite where Oprah once stayed. It was larger than my house and had two master suites and a balcony that looked out onto the world. Needless to say, we ate in the room that night. What a feeling to be expecting one thing that is not so very great at all and then be given an upgrade beyond all expectation.

Let me advance this point before moving on. I went on a field trip with my daughter's class to Europe. Her choir was competing there, and I wanted to have some special dad-daughter time. I travel a lot, and my worst nightmare is to be in a cramped coach seat on a twelve-hour flight over the ocean. I get squeamish just thinking about it. But I wanted to go on the trip, so with all the courage I had within me, I boarded the plane and took my place in the little seat that made me feel very sorry for sardines. The trip was more cramped, more crowded, and longer than I imagined. With great relief I walked off that plane in London.

We had a good trip, but every day there I lived with the dread of the trip home. It was a little dark cloud hanging over my head as I reviewed every restless moment on the way over. I had no fear of flying; I had a fear of stuffing myself back in that seat.

When the trip was over and we went through all the searches and security checks, we ended up in the waiting area of the airport. Above the rumble of all the excited kids looking forward to the flight of movies, snacks, pranks, and naps, I heard my name called. I walked to the desk and was handed a new boarding pass with a seat assignment in first class. I immediately thought someone sent them a movie of me on the way over, and they decided to have pity on me. It was a mercy upgrade. But that was not the case. They just had too many people show up for coach and went down the alphabet for whom to upgrade, and Arterburn came up first. You cannot imagine how great I felt to receive that upgrade.

Living the Upgrade

But better than getting the upgrade was living the upgrade. In first class on Virgin Atlantic they give massages, serve gourmet food, and have seats that lie flat so you can sleep on little mattresses. It was the exact opposite of the experience in coach. It was luxury to the max and turned my trip into something I will never forget. That is what an upgrade can do for anyone who receives one.

But upgrades don't have to be limited to hotels and airplanes. They can occur in your life. And the good news is you don't have to wait for someone else to put you in a better place. You can determine to experience life in a whole new way, leaving behind any misery or desperation.

If you have been sitting back in the coach section of the plane in seat SHAME4U, wouldn't you want to upgrade the emotion of shame and replace it with acceptance, forgiveness, compassion, and hope? Aren't those upgrades much better than sitting in your own shame?

If you are back there sitting every day in IBANGRY, you can upgrade to feelings of understanding, forgiveness, acceptance, love, and patience. What a wonderful upgrade in life.

If your seat is IFEAR2, you can upgrade that emotion and live in confident peace, able to trust and accept the vulnerabilities of life. You can upgrade any emotion and live with a different state of mind if you are willing to do the work to earn the upgrade. The hard work is always worth it. Don't you want to live the upgraded life?

Some people can have the upgrade, but they refuse it. If they were offered one on my plane, they might have resisted because they did not think they deserved it or someone would think they wasted money on it. Or they might not want to be separated from the people they were used to being with. In real life, there are also those who refuse to move up to a better emotional level of functioning. They don't want to pay the price, or they are unwilling to try living in an uncomfortable and uncertain style. But if people are willing, they can resolve their issues and find a way to live the emotional upgrade that is available to all of us.

Porch Parenting

In the introduction I briefly mentioned a man who decided to emotionally upgrade his life. It was a tragic story of abandonment and desertion of an infant by a very sick mother. As this young man grew up, he was entitled to hang on to any anger, bitterness, or sadness he wanted, but he decided to trade all that in on a new way of feeling and living. He chose to upgrade his life. If you try to put yourself in his place, you may find some area of your life that needs an emotional upgrade, and you might courageously decide, as he did, you want to live at a different level.

Imagine what it would be like for a small boy with no father to be taken next door to the neighbors and left by his mother—left with no note or good-bye or explanation. This boy lived through years of bitterness and resentment toward a mother he never knew as a child. He had learned to survive, but he was in the workshop because although he tried to convince himself he was getting along just fine, he was full of negativity and wanted to feel better.

Ironically, the day before the workshop began, his mother

found him, made contact, and wanted to connect with him and be part of his life. Imagine, after not even knowing if your mother was alive or dead, twenty years later from out of nowhere she shows up in your life wanting to take her place as your mother and share your life.

Whatever anger, hurt, and bitterness had been suppressed for so many years welled up within him. He wanted to hit her or at least shake her and tell her of all the misery he endured because she abandoned him. He rejected her offer to reconcile and demanded she not contact him again.

On the first night of the workshop he revealed to the group what happened. He shared his dismay and shock at the thought of a woman he vilified all his life now wanting to be a happy family member. If there was any good in this woman who forsook him, he couldn't imagine it.

The group heard his description of a woman he never met in person and it was all bad. He was hurting deeply and in tears when he finished. Everyone expressed his or her understanding of the deep hurt that came from being abandoned by his mother, which compounded the hurt of not knowing his father.

On a hunch I asked him if he would be willing to do something very difficult and painful but that might lead to the beginning of a whole new life. He was willing. I told him that after the session was over, I wanted him to contact his mother. He told me he could and would. I asked him to ask her about what happened in her childhood and report back to the group the next day. I wanted him to discover the most hurtful thing she had been through and then share that with the group.

The next morning we saw a very different man come to the session. There was no look of rage on his face or sounds of fury coming from his mouth. He was calm and seemed to be at peace, but he had two of the most bloodshot eyes I have ever seen. I could not wait to find out what happened.

I called on him to report to the group what he did and what he was told. While having difficulty holding back tears, he told the group he called his mother and asked her about her childhood. What he discovered changed his life forever. She told him she never really knew her father and one day her mother, who was prone to vast mood swings of deep depression and outbursts of rage, took her next door to the neighbor's house and left her there. And she never, ever came back.

She explained she did the same thing out of desperation, hoping he would never have to see her out of control or, much worse, be the victim of one of her attacks. So, while he was still an infant she took him next door, hoping the neighbors would give him a better life than she could. She told him of praying for him every day and hoping that unlike her own mother, she would be able to come back and be part of his life.

Hearing this, he immediately realized his mother was not evil. She simply did what she learned from her mother. And it was not him specifically she rejected; more accurately, she rejected the concept of a child, not the person he would one day become. But more precisely, it was an act of protection more than desertion, and her motive was for him to have a better life.

With these new understandings in mind, he began to reframe the entire incident, giving up resentment and anger and trading them in for the beginnings of love and even admiration. It was the beginning of his recovery from the deep wounds that drove his life and controlled his destiny. With the new facts he reframed his past and that motivated him to resolve what he reframed. Without reframing his mother, he never would have resolved his feelings toward her.

The Process That Leads to Resolution

I have written entire books on this process of resolution. *Healing Is a Choice* and *Transformation* take different looks at the process and both can help you when you are ready to resolve whatever it is you have reframed. For the purposes of this book, I want to present some resolution concepts that could help you move on and out of the areas that have held you captive. I have created a list of actions. I hope you can take these steps with someone else who can guide and encourage you along the way. These are actions you can use as a pathway for recovery or a guide in your therapy. Look at what you are doing to heal and determine whether or not these elements are there. If you are just getting started, be sure to include all of them in your journey.

1. Examination: Become a student of your own life. Take a look at the patterns that have developed. Plot the course you most often take when things become uncomfortable. Look for the places where you hold the most negative emotions. What do you feel most often: Is it anger? Guilt? Fear?

Start to look at yourself and your life objectively so you can develop a plan to resolve the areas of emotional contamination that keep you entrenched in the past and in darkness.

2. *Openness and confession:* As our lives become focused on the horrible things others have done to us, we lose sight of our own problems. Those we do see, we hide so no one will know just how sick or in need we are. We come to live in a cesspool of our own sins. In order to come out of that, we need to risk becoming open about the struggles we are going through. We also need to confess the sins we are involved with. We need a change from hiding and hunkering down to a willingness to open up and confess. That way we do not have to carry any additional shame with us.

3. *Focus on now:* Whatever happened in the past is over and done with. You cannot change it, you can only channel it. That means you take whatever pain you lived through and channel the power of it into something meaningful today. Today you are a survivor. Today you are living with many gifts, talents, strengths, and gadgets. You must refuse to ruminate about the past that is over and wake up to the life you have now, focusing on the opportunities before you.

4. *Choosing to forgive:* I don't know of a tougher choice to make than the choice to forgive. I also don't know of another choice with as many rewards. There is no resolution without forgiveness. We are commanded to forgive others as God has forgiven us. It is not an option to forgive if we feel like it. We just have to do it. And it seems so unfair to have to deal with the pain of what people have done to us and then go through the pain of forgiving them for doing it. They soil our slates with their misdeeds, and then we are asked to wipe their slates clean. It is so difficult that some never do it, and some don't think it is possible.

I have often been confronted by victims of abuse who really believe they must not forgive. Some believe that if they forgive, they will allow the same thing to happen to them again. Some believe they don't have to forgive unless the other person repents. Some won't forgive unless it is specifically asked for.

But I believe what the other person does is irrelevant. We need to forgive and free ourselves from the despicable events of the past the perpetrator and abuser cause. It won't come easily or instantly, but the sooner we begin, the sooner we can forgive and live free of the influence from the evil done to us.

The forgiveness process also involves another person other than the one who hurt us. It must also be given to the one who was hurt. We must forgive ourselves. We must offer ourselves the grace we give others and the grace God gives us. We must not beat ourselves up and shame ourselves over and over for something we cannot change or undo. To resolve all areas of our lives, we must be willing to let go of the self-condemnation we have felt we deserved and we rationalized made things better in some way. Nothing is made better when we live hating ourselves for our mistakes. We must find a way to forgive the sins done to and by us and be ready to forgive the sins we will surely face in our future.

5. *Choosing to let go:* If there is anything more difficult than forgiving, it is choosing to let go. Choosing to let go is the act of turning your life and will over to God. It is giving up control that makes us feel so important and keeps us distracted from doing the painful things we need to do to heal and transform our lives. Letting go is trusting God for the results. It is work-

ing even though we may not yet see the end result of our work. It is a willingness to risk not having to be in charge of every moment of our lives.

For many of us who have been taught and trained to take control, letting go is never easy, but it is one of the most powerful acts of faith. It is an open acknowledgment of our faith in God. And more than any other action, it allows us to rest, be at peace, and know a life of serenity.

6. *Making amends and restitution:* Perhaps this is the most frequently neglected action in the process of resolving the issues of life. We certainly want people to pay a price if they hurt us. We don't want someone to ruin our lives and walk away scot-free. We want someone to pay for our suffering. We want to see a sacrifice that shows they are sincere in their remorse and sorrow.

By the same token, others want and deserve that from us. If we have betrayed, we need to figure out what we can do to pay for the betrayal. Of course nothing will totally make up for what we have done, but making amends, asking for forgiveness, saying "I am sorry," paying back money taken, replacing damaged goods, or giving up a luxury item because of what you took from someone else can help you feel forgiven and live knowing you did everything you could to make up for the loss and pain you caused.

7. *Making a plan to protect yourself:* Resolving your emotional traumas and conflicts takes a lot out of you. If you try too hard and are not paying attention, when you least expect it you can fall back into your old ways. You build up the old resentments and repeat the same patterns that keep you stuck.

When you protect yourself, you are less likely to have a relapse and get off the track toward purpose and meaning. You protect yourself with healthy people in social settings. You find more protection by going to your small group and getting to know the members and letting them in on who you are.

Protection comes from always having a healthy place to go. It might be the lobby of a therapist's office or a local codependency group meeting at Celebrate Recovery or Al-Anon.

Protection is a healthy sign of humility. It acknowledges that you are not brilliant enough to know when you may be vulnerable to relapse. It protects you from your past and protects you from repeating all the mistakes you have made up to this point.

8. *Fulfilling the dream of reaching others:* Life really is not all about you. In the world of the clinically obsessed, it is hard to find a way to authentically reach out to others without getting in the way of yourself. It is easy to stumble from trauma into meaninglessness. We need to begin looking, early on, at how we can reach out to others. We need to secure our own progress by assisting others in their programs of healing. It is in this action we find meaning and purpose and a desire to go on living and contributing to a world that needs everyone to contribute.

These are the actions you can take to resolve all that has been troubling you. They are steps on a different path from most people's. They move you beyond just seeing things differently; they motivate you to live life to the fullest.

Living a life that resolves the issues of the past is not an easy one, but it is much easier than any of the other consequences of not resolving and getting on with your life. There are those situations where we think it could not be any worse or dreadful or painful than what we have endured. We may have known for years we needed to resolve something. Then, just when we are ready to resolve it all, the perpetrator is found dead in his apartment. If this is what has happened or this is what you fear, there is hope.

Worst-Case Scenario

You might have been in a similar situation to the man who was left on the front porch by his inadequate mother. Your mother didn't come back to tell you that what she did was really out of love. There are no new facts to be revealed so you can see whoever hurt you in a new and different light. And you may think that since there is nothing new to be discovered, no "emotional upgrade" is going to fall in your lap. You feel stuck and even a bit jealous of a man who had a parent care enough to come back around. If that is your case, there really is still hope.

Let's say you have lived with the residue of a sick father who not only sexually molested you but was an admired church leader. To everyone but you, he was a man of integrity who worked hard, provided for the family that looked perfect, and not only went to church but taught Sunday school. His only problem was creeping into your room at night, fondling you, telling you he loved you, that you were special, and that you must keep this little secret to yourself or your mother would go crazy, hate you, and everything the family has would be lost. It was all up to you to keep it all together.

You had to endure the abuse and sacrifice yourself for the rest of the family. And just when you got old enough to want to do something about the past, he up and died one day, leaving you with the secret.

You will never hear an apology or confession or watch him be carried off to jail for the felony he committed against you. You will never get to tell him that for every moment of sick pleasure, you have endured hours upon hours of anger, grief, horror, fear, and suicidal depression. You are left holding the bag you have been dragging around since the nightmare started.

How does someone in this situation upgrade to another level? How does someone struggling alone with this kind of secret find the way to a new way of feeling and living? It is difficult but possible. You have to go back to the five roadblocks at the beginning of the book and work through any of them that are keeping you from living the reframed life. Then, without a need for a response from anyone else, begin to work through the actions that will lead you down the path toward resolution.

When Is It Resolved?

If resolution is the goal, how do you know you have finally achieved it? You have achieved the goal when something that was a dominating, negative influence in your life no longer has any power over you. You remember what happened, but you don't relive the pain when you think back on it. The bad event is not taking anything away from your life and, in fact, has added something to it because you have learned so much from going through the reframing and resolving processes.

You don't hold a grudge against but instead have some sympathy for the person who hurt you, or at least you pity him or her for the life in which he or she is stuck. You see the abuser's sickness and have risen above it. You realize you have grown from all that has happened, and you will not repeat the trauma inflicted upon you. You are better, stronger, and wiser for what you have been through and you view it as something that is in your past, something you have conquered.

CHAPTER THIRTEEN

From Reframing to Resolving to Refocusing Your Life

A New View of the Future

In my own life, when I am in the middle of a crisis, I have a pretty dismal view of the future. It is mostly full of fear, anxiety, and dread. I reach a point where I don't think I can take any more and will do anything to avoid feeling more pain or enduring another struggle. I see only the doom and gloom hovering around my life. If there is an upside, I can't see it and don't believe it is there.

As I begin to reframe what has happened and then start to work on resolving it, the view of the future begins to change. Little slivers of hope start to pierce the darkness, and I begin to believe God will make a way for me to survive and perhaps once again restore my soul.

It is a tough time when the future looks so bleak, but it does not stay that way for long. Eventually I work through whatever has happened, take back my life, and no longer live in fear and dread of another battle. I reach a point where I can see struggle as the substance for a purposeful future. History helps me see that. Every struggle I have been through has helped me help others who are still in the middle of theirs. I have gained new insights and much deeper compassion for those who are going through battles of their own.

I know my life is becoming refocused when I begin to normalize the difficulties I have to face. I see them as part of a normal life, and I don't catastrophize the outcome of the difficulties I face. I settle back into the routine of good days and not-so-good days with a problem or two and some greater than others. But no day feels as if it might be the end of the world. I gain a sense that I am going to survive and life is going to get better, but it will never be free of struggle and I do not expect it to be easy.

Eyes Forward

As my feelings settle down, I start to look to the future. My thoughts turn from regretting what happened and obsessing over why it happened and how I could have prevented it—to a different way of thinking. I start to realize that I have some strengths that have helped me get through it all. I have some insights that keep me from giving up. I have some new experiences that will connect me to some people I might not have made a connection with before. I start to think in terms of how I can use these things in the future to reach others rather than turn back toward a past I cannot change. I trust God wants me to use every ounce of pain and agony I have been through. I don't want to waste anything I have experienced.

The evidence of healing and resolution is a change of focus. I spend less time on me and what I look like than on others and what they are going through. It does not happen all at once, but this awareness kind of creeps up on me until one day I notice I am no longer taking up so much of my thoughts. I also feel love for others again. It is hard for me to feel that love when I am in so much pain I don't know if I can survive, but it comes back when I am well into healing and feeling the resolution of what I have been through.

Some would say that real Christians should feel that way from the beginning. From the moment they feel pain, they should be able to get totally out of themselves and into others. They should have peace and, because of their faith, be able to move on from the pain. I am aware of a ministry that believes that if any pastor goes through depression, it is an indication he is not fit to lead and must be replaced. There is room only for positive human emotion that is focused on others at all times.

I think that might be a reason there are so many problems in ministries. I think it pushes a person into denial, and then the consequences come crashing down. I think God understands us and how we function. There is surely acceptance for the process I have to go through to return to wholeness. I wish it was as easy as just talking or praying or believing, but it is not for me. To reframe and resolve and then to refocus my life is a process I wish I did not have to endure, but it is. That process always brings me to a place where I am ready to move on and move toward others.

Choosing the Point of Focus

Life can be a lot like taking pictures. I have just discovered the world of photography, and I love it. When Madeline and I were asked to go to Africa with Compassion International, I bought a great camera because they told us we would go on a couple of safaris in addition to the work we would be doing there. I wasn't a great photographer, but because the camera was digital, I could take as many pictures as I wanted, hoping by accident one of them was a real keeper. Most were not.

But one of the things that became clear to me is that what I chose to focus on put everything else out of focus. Actually, the way it worked was pointing the camera at a specific object and then the automatics in the little computer inside adjusted all the variables to that object, and after taking more than one thousand pictures, ten of them made me look like a genius photographer.

Too bad we can't operate our lives like a digital camera and just delete the snapshots of our lives that don't turn out as we wanted. We have to live with what we frame up as we focus on what we believe is important or significant.

If someone is fifty years old and still waiting for a seventy-five-year-old man to apologize for childhood neglect so she can get on with her life, then obviously the focus has been on the wrong thing. The focus has been on what happened and the person who did it. In the beginning, that is where the focus needs to be. That is where everything begins and ends because it is so much of a person's life. It has to be resolved, and you can't resolve it without focusing on it for a portion of your life—but not all of your life.

You have to move on. At some point you have to take your

eyes off the past and the abusive person and turn them over to God for help. You have to focus on God's grace for you, and you have to focus on who can help you get inside yourself and root out any emotional rot that is spreading there. Then you can shift your focus away from the incident and the perpetrator and turn your focus to taking what happened and making the best of it.

Making the Best of It

This really does sum up our main mission in life. It is our job to make the best of whatever happened to us. Many things that can happen to us are not from the cruelty of others, the punishment of God, or a result of our own mistakes. The fact is, very horrible things can happen in this world, and they are no one's fault. They just happen, and we are assigned the task of making the best of them, no matter what.

For instance, one of the toughest losses is having an arm or a leg amputated due to an accident or an illness. It is an instant reframing of the physical body of the amputee and the injured person must work his way through some very tough emotions to focus on a meaningful future.

In the photographic mind, the amputee can take a close-up of a stump with all of its weirdness and never move beyond it. The focus can be on how clothes fit over the severed limb or the scars that are left for others to grimace at. In the beginning, all those points of focus are normal—but not for long and not forever. The amputee must place these things in the background and focus on other parts of the body that remain whole and healthy. The shift must progress away from the accident and toward a healthy and even happy life.

Each of us has the free choice of what we will focus on. If we were raised to be whiners in life, we will always focus on what makes our lives uncomfortable and what others are not doing to make it better for us. We whine because somehow our focus is always on ourselves, our discomfort, our rights, and our tough circumstances. We feel we are arrogantly entitled to a life of ease or at least one that is easier, and until it shows up, we will focus on all the things that prove it has not shown up yet. What a miserable way to live!

If that is the way we live, we can move beyond it. We can change what we focus on. We can ask for and work on achieving patience we have never experienced before. Our determination to get what we deserve, or at least to point it out and express our disappointment over it, can be replaced with a new determination to take whatever we have and do something spectacular with it.

We have to change from a willingness to see only ourselves and our difficulties to a willingness to make the best lives for ourselves out of the worst things that have happened to us. Then one day, perhaps we can focus on helping others make the best of the worst things that have happened in their lives. First, we have to change our focus in our own lives.

If we are divorced, we need to make the best of it and learn from it. How did we pick someone who would leave us? How did we live in a deteriorating situation unaware? How do we learn all we can from it? How can we grow from it?

Finally, how can we take what we have been through and use it to help others deal with whatever they are going through? How can we make the best of it by reaching out to others who have been in the same situation and have done nothing beneficial with their lives? How can we help someone who continues to experience the consequences of poor decisions, poor connections, and a lack of willingness to get better?

When the focus is changed to these questions at the right time, life returns to a place of purpose and meaning. For most, it has even more purpose after the trauma has been resolved than it would have if the trauma had never occurred. But it takes a willingness to work with God in creating a life that benefits from all the things meant to destroy you.

Winning the Prize

When we change our focus from the past to the future and from our hurts to helping others, there is a great reward for the hard work required in making that radical shift in focus. The prize is transcending the past. That is prize enough. Getting out of the past that cannot be changed, has nothing good to offer us, and keeps us locked up in fear and anger can give us a present and a future that are nothing like the past. We can build new lives, and the Bible encourages us to do just that. Perhaps the most specific biblical insight and instruction on doing this is found in the third chapter of Philippians:

> But one thing I do: Forgetting what is behind and straining toward what is ahead, I press on toward the goal to win the prize for which God has called me heavenward in Christ Jesus. (3:13–14 NIV)

When I read that passage, I take it to mean this: If there is one thing I am going to do with my life, it is not repeating my past. I am going to take what has happened to me and use that to make me a better husband, father, friend, and follower of Christ. It won't be easy, but with the help of God's power I am going to rip myself away from my past and its unhealthy patterns and move toward what lies ahead. With all I am and all I can do, I am going to find what I can do here on Earth to honor my God. I am going to work here to do what I can to help others, but I am always aware that one day I will be in heaven for eternity, where the struggle will be over and I will experience the rest of my life enjoying the prize that God is waiting to give me.

This is how I believe God wants me to focus my life today. And just like the camera that has all of those automatics inside that make it work, I have some too. I have what I have been taught, what I have been through, and the wise counsel of those around me to place the focus where it needs to be.

The New Thing

The refocused life gives up the old ways of doing things to experience a new thing. The refocused life gives up self-obsession and replaces it with an orientation toward others, connecting with fellow strugglers and comforting them in the same way you have been comforted. Your new purpose can become a daily source of amazement to you. You wake up and set out to defend someone who is in great need, and you realize you were once defenseless. You set out to help others, and you are overwhelmed with how far you have come from your days of helplessness. Out of some very crummy stuff, a new thing has emerged, and it is a wonderful life you never dreamed could have so much to offer you and others.

When this new thing happens, you are aligning yourself with what God wants for you. You are also aligning yourself with what God wants for others. You are his tool to help others, and he wants to use you if you will allow him to do so. Your willingness lines you up exactly where God wants you standing, or better said, stooping to help others.

This new thing also aligns you with the very character of God. He has been doing this with us since the beginning of time. The book of Isaiah puts it this way:

> See, I am doing a new thing!
> Now it springs up; do you not perceive it?
> I am making a way in the desert
> and streams in the wasteland. (43:19 NIV)

God is doing a new thing in your life, and you experience it because you allow him to do it. You also get to experience it in others because that new thing propels you to share your new life of hope and meaning with others. If you have not experienced that new thing, that turnaround, that refocused life, it might be helpful to go back to the beginning of the book. Look at the roadblocks to reframing and determine if one or more of those are preventing you from moving on to this new thing that is springing up, making streams of hope and purpose where there was once a wasteland of ugly despair and hopelessness.

Resetting Your Internal Automatics

The good news for those who get through the roadblocks is that you can reset the internal automatics or the default settings within you so you remain focused on the areas that will move your life forward. A reframed life takes a radical turn when the focus turns from all that was and will never be again to what remains and what can be restored—and how all of that can be used to help others restore the "lost years of the locust" (Joel 2:25). You can believe in your own weaknesses and inadequacies, or you can start to reset those automatic beliefs and replace them with awareness that the apostle Paul pointed us to in his letter to the Philippians in the fourth chapter:

I have strength for all things in Christ Who empowers me. [I am ready for anything and equal to anything through Him Who infuses inner strength into me; I am self-sufficient in Christ's sufficiency.] (v. 13 AMP)

This passage is not a nice quote to help you feel better about yourself. So often that is how verses like this are treated. This is more than just a great-sounding set of words. It puts our focus on what is within us as believers. This is a powerful truth that is underutilized and underlived. According to this Scripture, you can accomplish what you want to get done for God. You can find the future you have been wanting. You do not have to remain weak and wandering. God has given you strength.

Peter says we not only have strength, but through God we have everything we need:

His divine power has given us everything we need for life and godliness through our knowledge of him. (1:3 niv)

this and live like this, or
elves from future stress,
ike another disappoint-
strength to withstand
in our knowledge of
to action. The more
al automatics to be

fe without mention-
nd too few use. For
n when they finally
gifts God has given
e these gifts for him,
e, and a lot of pieces

angry and depressed
dad was never there
y. Then when his dad
Contrast that with the
dad into the emotion-
ildhood and so poorly
lves his anger and rises
the focus from himself
cess, he discovers gifts,
he had.

m to minister to others
r and in the process finds
and happiness than he

ever imagined possible. I believe that is possible for anyone who reframes, resolves, refocuses, and utilizes the gifts God has given him or her.

God has given us these amazing gifts, yet many never try to discover or develop them. But God has given them to us for a reason. First of all, we have to realize that they are truly gifts. There is nothing we did to earn them. They are undeserved, unmerited, and given to be given away. First Corinthians 12:7 tells us these gifts are given to us "for the common good" (NIV). They are not for us to use to rack up accomplishments; we are to use them for the good of others rather than self-edification, self-discovery, or self-promotion. It is so easy to see how broken people who discover their gifts can make those gifts all about self rather than about someone else. The bottom line is that we are to exercise these gifts with great love. We are instructed in 1 Corinthians 13, the love chapter not to be self-seeking, rude, impatient, unkind, grudging, or envious. We are simply to love others and use these gifts to minister to them out of love.

Ephesians 4:12–13 tells us God wants us to use our gifts to spread his grace, truth, guidance, and healing. If we don't use what we have, people starving for God's truth will never hear it. Those who need to know God is full of grace may view him only as angry and uncaring. The emotionally, spiritually, and physically sick may not find healing if we who have gifts don't use them. How sad to go through life with the capacity to be an instrument of God and never know you could be or get involved in the very reason you were placed on the earth.

Jesus did not just die for the church and the body of believers within it. He provided a way to meet needs by giving all of us sharable gifts. He prepares us to do the work that needs to be done so the church, the body of Christ, can be built up and strengthened. God wants a mature church, experiencing the whole measure of fullness in Christ. Show me a church where people are using their gifts, and most likely they don't have time to split over minor issues because they are so busy serving. They don't criticize the paid staff because they all see themselves as unpaid staff, all called to serve and minister within the body of Christ. A church where people are using their gifts is a church on fire, and that fire can be ignited by the excitement of one person who finally discovers the gifts God has for her and begins to develop and use them for the greater good of the body of Christ.

You could be the very person who has been called to ignite that fire in your home church. If so, your life will be focused on the right stuff if you will respond to what you have been called to do. Say yes to God and watch what God will do with your willingness.

Not Just Another List

Following is a list of gifts from the Bible. It isn't just another list to look at to see if you find anything interesting about it. On this list you could find your future. You could find what God has called you to do uniquely and powerfully. Take a look and see if you think there are some gifts you need to unwrap, pull out of the box, and use in your newly refocused life.

First Corinthians 12 presents us with the following list:

1. Wisdom—a gift of imparting wisdom beyond your years because you are able to see deeply into situations and understand all the angles of a problem and its solution.
2. Knowledge—a gift that allows you to say something that helps people clarify what they are struggling with or a path they need to take.
3. Faith—a gift that keeps you steady in your dependence on the Lord in the toughest times, when others falter under the pressure.
4. Healing—a gift of saying the right thing, prescribing the right treatment, or being able to influence the disease process through your special touch. (I don't think it happens very often in front of a stadium full of people but rather when someone is hurting deeply and all alone.)
5. Miraculous powers—a gift to do what is humanly impossible to do. This could be something so obvious as knowing what another person is saying even though you do not know his language or being able to do some miraculous feat in assisting someone else.
6. Prophecy—a gift that allows you to proclaim God's message in a way that people respond. You can see people's needs and know how to communicate in a way that reaches them.
7. Discernment between spirits—a gift that enables you to determine if someone or something has an evil, hidden agenda.
8. Tongues—the gift of speaking in an unknown prayer language.
9. Interpretation of tongues—the ability to understand what that person means when he speaks in that prayer language.

There are other gifts listed in these three other passages: Romans 12:6–8, Ephesians 4:11–13, 1 Peter 4:10–11.

10. Service—a gift of knowing what others need and being able to minister to them.
11. Teaching—a gift of being able to communicate God's truths in a way that people can understand, enjoy, and apply.
12. Encouraging—a gift of knowing how to cheer up people or to help them see the upside of their difficulties.
13. Contributing to the needs of others—being able to give so that others can get by. Some say this gift of giving is "the gift of getting so you can give."
14. Leadership—a gift that fosters loyalty and enables you to understand what needs to be developed and implemented to accomplish a goal by motivating others to help.
15. Showing mercy—a gift of being aware of other's needs and being able to communicate love and acceptance from Christ.
16. Apostleship—a gift of serving as one who is called to work directly for the Lord in or outside a church, drawing others to Christ.
17. Evangelism—a gift to win others to Christ.
18. Pastoring—the gift of leading a church.
19. Speaking—the gift of communication that inspires and enlightens those who listen.

Simple Discovery Indicators

If you want to know all of your gifts, there are some great surveys and quizzes that can help you with your discovery. You can Google *spiritual gifts* and find some great places to

take these. I have a simple checklist to help guide your thinking as you consider what gifts God may have given you. Look
at these four principles in discovering what one of your gifts
might be:

1. It is something I like to do.
2. Others agree I'm good at this.
3. I execute it with supernatural ease or brilliance.
4. I have complementary natural skills.

That is a pretty simple checklist, but for a lot of people
it helps to uncover some gifts they did not know they had. I
think I have the gift of speaking. First of all, I love to speak. I
mean, when it goes well I love to speak. But that in itself is an
indication I have this gift. I know when it does and does not
go well. Contrast that with some of the people who audition
for *American Idol*. They actually think they can sing, and they
have no talent whatsoever. When I speak well, I am on top of
the world.

Others agree I'm good at speaking. I was placed in the National Speakers Hall of Fame. I once received a ten-minute
standing ovation I cried through. Churches and pastors like
Rick Warren ask me to fill in for them. After I speak, people
say it impacts them deeply.

And it is easy for me to do. I have a formula I stick to, and
if you need me to speak in a few minutes, I have a formula that
will enable me to deliver a pretty good talk.

Finally, I have complementary natural skills. I can write, so
the way I speak is coupled with strong truth. I am an athlete,
so I can endure the grinds of speaking. I have a sense of humor

and have listened to the greatest comedians perform and developed my own timing.

It all fits together to convince me that my speaking is much more a result of God gifting me than my learning to do it better than others. I am sorry if this sounds like bragging. I don't mean to. My hope is that you will look at your life, discover a gift or two as I did, and enjoy using and developing it.

CHAPTER FOURTEEN

Leaving You with a Promise

When the concept for this book came to mind, I began to see all I wanted to communicate in hopes of making an impact on your life. I developed the material during a couple of years and then I put it together within a six-month period that was a time of great change for me. My son, Solomon, was born in the middle of the writing, and his birth made this book even more meaningful to me.

I began to think of it within the context of his birth and life ahead. The writing took a turn into what I would want him to know that was truly important. I began to think of what I would want to leave behind for him if I were in an accident or died of a heart attack like my father. The book became more important to me than others I have written. I am trying to talk to you the way I hope to talk with my son someday. It is an attempt to deliver vital information on how to live life if I am not around to teach him in person.

Now, at the close of the book, I am writing it as if it were the last chapter I will ever write. I want to leave you with words I hope you will remember and a few last concepts I hope will continue to make a difference in your life. To that end, I want to leave you with three things: a quote, a verse, and a promise.

A Quote to Remember

I don't want to say that I am old, but having passed fifty a few years back, I have to admit I am growing older. When you find yourself on the other side of fifty, some things you held on to so tightly are not so important anymore. Or at least you see them much differently. You tend to focus less on the minor things and start to spend your time dealing with the priorities or essentials in life. When that happens, you change and move on in your thinking. If you are maturing as God would have you mature, your life becomes less and less about you and more and more about others. You do not wake up every morning looking for new proof that the world is revolving around you. Instead, you begin to have much higher priorities. Those priorities are the needs and desires of others. Albert Camus put it this way:

To grow old is to pass from passion to compassion.

When I hear a judgmental person condemning someone without knowing what is really going on in that person's life, I realize that while the critical individual may have gotten older, he or she has not gotten wiser or moved from being so passionate about a single thing to become much more compassionate about the lives of others. One of the greatest acts of reframing is the movement from self-centeredness to an other-person focus.

If that is all you accomplish through reading this book, it will change everything about your life. Getting out of yourself and into others is the reframing God has called all of us to do. But in doing that, he has not ignored us or left us without a way of dealing with our own struggles and painful difficulties.

A Verse to Live By

All of us are on a journey together as we make our way through this world full of mystery and wonder. We come into the world genetically wired and we are raised by people who work with the wiring, strengthening some of the connections and weakening others. We grow and learn and eventually discover we are responsible to do what we can to live successfully in spite of any wiring problems that make living difficult.

The temptation for any of us is to stop moving forward and comfortably stagnate in a predictable world that appears to be less painful. If we succumb to that temptation, our vision becomes very impaired and we develop a nearsightedness that focuses only on our pain and blinds us to the hope and promise that we can experience in the future—if we will trek out of the rut of our painful memories and regrets.

We will never start the trek if we are able only to see life in the context of our own pain. We will not move out into meaningful lives if all we care about is how badly we have messed up or been hurt. We will miss what we were designed for if all we can do is relive the past and wait for justice to be done to others or punishment from God to finally ruin whatever hope and potential we had left.

The reframed life has moved beyond a dismal rut where only the downside of life is seen, felt, and lived. The reframed life is the life God wants us to live so we can finish strong with him in control and our reaching out to others as our meaningful purpose and focus.

The psalmist pointed us toward this kind of life in Psalm 84. The passage reads:

> Blessed are those whose strength is in you,
> who have set their hearts on pilgrimage.
> As they pass through the Valley of Baca (weeping),
> they make it a place of springs. (vv. 5–6 NIV)

In this simple passage I see the ultimate context for reframing everything in life. First of all, we see we are blessed or gifted when we are relying on God's strength and not our own. That is a dramatic new way to move into the future. Stop trying to prove you have what it takes to accomplish anything you want and accept that you don't. Instead, daily ask God to be your source of strength and worship him by turning every area of your life over to him. Ask him to help you step up and accept responsibility but, more importantly, ask him to help you step aside when you need to allow him to do for you what you cannot do for yourself.

Life is good when God is our strength and we have set our hearts upon a pilgrimage. In God's strength, we are moving toward something better. We are on a journey, and all we are is focused on that pilgrimage toward something better. Our hearts are not set on the daily struggles we experience. Our hearts are not set on a past we cannot change because we are moving toward something far greater. It is a future of wholeness and healing, so we accept the challenge to keep on moving. This passage says if we have turned our lives over to God and are mindful that the pilgrimage is in process, we are to focus on it rather than on a detail along the way that might take us off the path.

Then this passage presents us with a vivid picture of what the reframed life can be: "As they pass through the Valley of Baca [weeping]—they make it a place of springs." If you are going through a rough time that feels like the valley of weeping described here, then be sure, as the passage says, you are passing through. If you have gotten stuck in the valley of weeping, the swamp of sadness, or the ocean of despair, just make your way right on out of there. Reframe what could be a place you never get out of to a temporary place you just happen to be in right now.

In the power of God you will take all the pain and suffering and turn it into a place of springs. You will create places of springs out of the driest moments of life. In other words, you will find life and get life and bring life to the worst parts of what you have been through. They will become the places you build on. They will add to your life rather than take away from it if you will live with the attitude of passing through the rough places rather than being willing to live in them, and more accurately, die in them. Through reframing, God wants to bring life to the dead places of your life.

A Promise to Hold Onto

About five seconds outside the womb, I think we all discover this life is not easy. The older we get, the tougher it becomes. Some seem to be smitten by problems beyond comprehension. Others seem to skate through life with little difficulty. Your path is going to be tough for you, and it does not matter whether or not it looks easier to others. Your pain sometimes makes you wonder if you are going to be able to make it through. You will if you hold on to the God who put you on that path. He has given us many promises, but I want to leave you with one that will allow you to stick around to live out all the other promises. Here is what he reveals to us in the book of Hebrews:

> I will not in any way fail you nor give you up nor leave you without support. [I will] not . . . in any degree leave you helpless. (AMP)

Rather than try to restate, clarify, or amplify that promise, I am just going to leave you with God's words. At any point, if you feel alone and without hope, use these words to reframe whatever you are going through, knowing that God will always be there for you.

Epilogue

Thank you for giving me your time and attention. I am so grateful you found this book. I am praying as I write the words that they have been and will be helpful to you. I would love to hear from you, so if you would like to contact me directly, you can do so by e-mailing me at:

SArterburn@newlife.com

There are many resources available to you at Newlife.com, or you can talk to someone by calling 1-800-Newlife. We have workshops that could help you as they have helped many others. These intensive experiences are called Healing Is a Choice, Lose It for Life, Reframe Your Life and Love. Also, please look at our radio station log at Newlife.com. You can find out where *New Life!* airs in your area or you can discover the times we are on Sirius and XM satellite radio.

About the Author

Stephen Arterburn is a bestselling author of more than seventy books with six million books in print. Several of his books have sold more than one million copies, including *The Life Recovery Bible* and *Every Man's Battle*. The Every Man series is now topping three million in sales. He is the recipient of three Gold Medallion Awards for writing excellence.

Stephen is the host of a syndicated radio talk show, *New Life!*, heard on more than 185 stations across the country. The one-hour live call-in program is known for bringing more new listeners to Christian radio than any other program. *New Life!* is also heard on Sirius and XM satellite radio twice each day.

Stephen is also a speaker, filling in for such pastors as Rick Warren of Saddleback Church and Chuck Smith Jr. of Calvary Chapel. He also speaks for Women's Resource Centers as a major fund-raiser and is a featured Promise Keepers speaker. Additionally he conducts weight loss and healing intensives and produces his own speaking events in cities where *New Life!* is broadcast.

Stephen has been featured on numerous national morning news programs such as *Good Morning America* and major talk shows, including three appearances on *Oprah*. He has been featured in national publications such as *USA Today*, the *New York Times*, *U.S. News & World Report*, *GQ*, and *Rolling Stone*.

Stephen is married to Misty. He is the father of the amazing soccer star Madeline and stepdad to two brilliant boys named James and Carter. On August 16, 2006, the amazing Solomon Russell Arterburn was born and soon became a very happy little baby full of a lot of love and laughter.

You can check all of this out at Newlife.com or contact Stephen at SArterburn@newlife.com.

NEW LIFE Ministries

Transforming Lives...
...Through God's Truth

New Life Ministries is a non profit organization, founded by author and speaker, Stephen Arterburn. Our mission is to identify and compassionately respond to the needs of those seeking healing and restoration through God's truth.

New Life's ministry of healing and transformation includes:

New Life! – Our daily, call-in counseling radio program hosted by Stephen Arterburn. To find a station near you call 1-800-NEW-LIFE or go to www.newlife.com. You can also listen online.

Counselors – Our network of over 700 counsleors nationwide. Call 1-800-New-Life to find one near you.

Weekend Intensive Workshops
- *Every Man's Battle*
- *Healing Is a Choice*
- *Lose It for Life*
- *Reframe Your Life*

Seminars
- *Reframing Your Life and Love*
- *Nights of Healing*

Coaching – Our personal coaching program is "Professional Accountability" to come alongside you and give you solution-focused direction.

Website
- Podcasts and broadcasts of **New Life!**
- Blogs, message boards and chats
- Our online store, featuring products by our radio show hosts
- Find workshops and counselors in your area

24-Hour Call Center – There is someone answering calls in our Call Center, 24 hours a day, 7 days a week, 365 days a year.

Reframe Your Life,
Healing Is a Choice and *Lose It for Life*
Weekend Intensives
with *New Life!* host, Steve Arterburn

Reframe Your Life

The Reframe Your Life, three-day intensive workshop is designed to help you see your life from a whole new perspective—you'll learn how to place a new frame around your past hurtful life experiences to help you recognize that God does allow and cause things to happen in your life for a reason. By reframing your past, it will give you the freedom to live your future free and turn those experiences around . . . almost like they were always meant to be. You'll see that some of your biggest challenges may truly become opportunities to love and serve others, and in the process . . . love and serve God.

Healing Is a Choice

If you are struggling with anger, depression, anxiety, grief and loss, divorce, abuse, marital struggles, are a wife whose husband is caught in sexual addiction, or are just feeling stuck in your emotional or spiritual state and need a breakthrough, then *Healing Is a Choice* is the workshop for you.

Lose It for Life

The *Lose It for Life* three-day intensive workshop is designed to address weight loss from an emotional and spiritual perspective without pressure, shame, condemnation or guilt. Let the flame of realistic, gentle, lifestyle change be kindled for you! "Jump-start" your journey into a free and full life by registering for our Lose It for Life workshop.

Every Man's Battle Workshop

The goal of the *Every Man's Battle* three-day workshop is to equip each man with the tools necessary to maintain sexual integrity and to enjoy healthy, productive relationships. By the completion of the program, attendees will have insight into the nature of sexual temptation and be able to use those tools to battle it.

Here is what people are saying...